BRIDGES TO AUTONOMY

Paradoxes in Teaching and Learning

Matthew R. Silliman
David Kenneth Johnson

Piraeus Books

Copyright © 2011 Piraeus Books LLC

First published in 2011 by Piraeus Books
P.O.Box 701, Williamstown, Massachusetts 01267
www.piraeusbooks.com

All rights reserved. No part of this book may be reprinted, reproduced, or stored in a retrieval system, without the permission of the publisher.

Library of Congress Control Number: 2011933634

Matthew R. Silliman & David Kenneth Johnson

Bridges to Autonomy: Paradoxes in Teaching and Learning

ISBN 9780983185383

Printed and bound in the United States of America

For our first and best teachers

June and Chuck Silliman

Connie and Ken Johnson

and the other inspired educators
who have shaped our lives and work.

Contents

Introduction:	**Between Bridges and the Reader**	vii
Chapter One:	**Between Authority and Autonomy**	1

Grumpy Faces
Problems of Paternalism
Grounding Paternalism

Interlude: Jules Randolph Govier

Chapter Two:	**Between Teaching and Learning**	25

What is Learning?
Learning Something as Knowing How
Lecture on Lectures
Consuming Learning
Between Knower and Known
Constructivist Realism

Interlude: Russell Steadman

Chapter Three:	**Between Neutrality and Justice**	47

Liberating Reason
The Politics of Teaching
Critical Thinking and Neutrality
Two Notions of Criticality

Interlude: Alison Bridges

Chapter Four:	**Between Structure and Creativity**	69

Creativity and Imagination
Educating Taste
Pedagogical Improvisations

Interlude: Jules Randolph Govier

Chapter Five:	**Between Showing and Telling**	91

A New Socratism?
Socratic Problems
Stories, Feelings, Reason
Teaching and Deception
Teachers as Tricksters

Interlude: Russell Steadman

Chapter Six:	**Between Content and Character**	119

Socratic "Values Education"?
Character and Intellectual Virtues
Indoctrination and Reason
Narrative Imagination and Felt Reasons
Educational Competition?

Interlude: Alison Bridges

Conclusion:	**Bridges to the Reader**	139

What's a Paradox?
Is Dialogue Really Philosophy?
Alternatives to Compulsory Schooling?
How Can We Become Ourselves?
Isn't Philosophy Competitive?
Memorization and *Creativity?*
Personal Strategies for Structural Problems?
To Teach or Not To Teach

Epilogue	155
Bibliography	157
Index	163

Introduction

Between Bridges and the Reader

Alison: Excuse me, but didn't we meet in this section of this bookstore a couple of years ago?

Reader: Yes, I remember you well. You're Alison Bridges from *Bridges to the World: A Dialogue on the Construction of Knowledge, Education, and Truth*. I read it in one sitting on a flight to Seattle.

Alison: I'm happy to hear that. What did you think?

Reader: It was a fun challenge. If someone had asked me before you convinced me to give it a try, I would not have thought that I could understand, much less enjoy, a book about the theory of knowledge. But the interplay between you and your friends kept it alive and accessible for me.

Alison: It was a great conversation, one that challenged me, too, and left me a better thinker and teacher.

Reader: I notice two of your friends, Jules and Russell, have returned to continue the dialogue. What's the topic this time around?

Alison: Imagine listening in on a conversation between your favorite teacher and some of her or his colleagues talking about their craft, its challenges, rewards, and prospects.

Reader: Would this be mainly about college teaching, or education generally?

Alison: While we presently work in high schools and universities, between the three of us we have taught at almost every level. There are some differences in application – certainly different approaches and content are appropriate at different ages – but I'm convinced that many of the basic principles and techniques are invariant across all levels of teaching.

Reader: I guess I can see that, since we're all just at different places on the same scale of development. So would this conversation settle questions about how to teach and why it matters?

Alison: It aims to discuss such questions, but it won't so much settle them as demonstrate how thoughtful and passionate people might explore them. It's up to the reader to decide whether the views and reasons expressed here are sufficient to settle anything. Many of the difficulties of teaching are not straightforward problems with simple solutions, but paradoxes we wrestle with endlessly.

Reader: What do you talk about specifically?

Alison: A full answer would take me all morning, but we tackle some thorny questions about what it means to know or understand something in an educational context; about how best to understand and promote the skills and habits of critical thinking; about the complexities of student autonomy and teacher directiveness; and about the nature and function of social-political critique in the classroom.

Reader: And do you talk at all about teachers themselves, and what makes some of them so effective and responsible?

Alison: Certainly, and in so doing we encounter some challenging ideas about the role of empathetic imagination in teaching, including the proper role of authority, irony, and clever misdirection as teaching strategies. It may turn out that teachers sometimes need to be tricksters.

Reader: I guess now I'll have to read the book to figure out what you mean by that. Pretty sneaky, throwing it in there.

Alison: Thank you.

Reader: I hear a lot these days from my conservative friends about "values education." Is this one of the other things your conversation addresses?

Alison: We try. I'm not sure my compatriots Russell and Jules have exactly the same understanding about what it means in practice, but we all seem to agree that character development is both an irreducible aspect of learning, and at the same time something we can never teach directly. We conclude that both moral and intellectual values are at the heart of education. I'd say your conservative friends are at least partially right about that.

Reader: This seems all very interesting, but I wonder whether teachers really need more philosophical, theoretical discussions like this. Maybe they just need a solid list of practical strategies.

Alison: Our conversation does touch on some practical approaches, but every one of them is in the end contestable. I'm sorry about this, really, but there are no magic bullets in teaching. The unpredictable, dialogical nature of any effective learning environment makes teaching more of an improvisational art than a science. Moreover, we're all philosophers to the extent that we think for ourselves about our work.

Reader: Fair enough. I like the idea of us each becoming our own philosophers or creative artists. We're all entitled to our own opinions, after all!

Alison: In one sense, that is certainly true. But contrary to popular assumption, philosophy is not essentially about opinions. Rather, it is about giving reasons, and listening closely to those you disagree with, in a shared effort to figure things out. It's not at all easy to do well, so you will find parts of this dialogue pretty challenging, despite our best efforts at clarity.

Reader: I understand. In recommending the book, you don't want to understate the difficulty of the subject, which is likely to persist despite the liveliness of the conversational form.

Alison: You took the words out of my mouth. With that kind of perceptivity, I have no doubt you will enjoy the book's challenges and profit from them.

Reader: Okay, Ms. Bridges, I'm just about convinced that I can handle this book, but I'm still a little worried. I've heard too many educational conversations devolve into gripe sessions about teachers' professional frustrations.

Alison: You correctly intuit that the nature of teachers' work makes frustration endemic. But suppose this conversation is ever so slightly idealized, so they can draw on texts and ideas from all over, and that their aim is not primarily to gripe, but rather to get a grip on basic principles behind their pedagogical choices.

Reader: That could be fun, like planting a hidden tape recorder in the faculty lounge on a really good day!

Alison: Something like that. You might get some insights about pedagogy, and at the same time a sense of how interesting it can be when a group of experienced, thoughtful friends address their difficulties together.

Reader: That last bit is more uncommon than we might expect in an allegedly advanced civilization.

Alison: Uncommon or not, here it is. If you like I could autograph the book for you after you buy it.

Reader: You can do that?

Alison: I don't think we've yet come anywhere near the limits of what literary and philosophical imagination can do.

Chapter One

Between Authority and Autonomy[1]

There is a perennial tension in teaching between one of its core purposes: empowering students to direct their own lives to a healthy degree – and one of its principal methods: to direct student thought and activity from a position of authority. Can teachers progressively engender student autonomy without employing errrantly paternalistic methods or assumptions?

Grumpy Faces

Jules: I'm so glad you two could meet me for coffee this morning. I'm sure every teacher sometimes experiences the kind of frustration I'm encountering, but I fear I'm at my wit's end. It's only the third week of the semester, but in some ways this is harder than when I used to teach middle-schoolers.

Alison: It's always good to get together with friends, Jules, especially at the foot of the Bridge of Flowers.[2] What exactly are you distressed about?

---

[1] 'Autonomy' in this conversation refers at once to the liberty of persons, their capacity to self-legislate, and to the thoughtful exercise of that liberty in a social context -- hence it emphasizes both individual maturity and healthy relationships with others.

[2] An abandoned trolley bridge on the Deerfield river that now serves as a linear garden and footbridge from Buckland to Shelburne Falls, Massachusetts.

Russell: Let me guess. After an initial burst of youthful energy, your students seem no longer thrilled at the prospect of learning anything. Am I close?

Jules: That's about the size of it. I think the worst thing is their facial expressions and body language. They look like grumpy zombies!

Alison: I'm familiar with that grumpy syndrome from painful experience. But how bad is it, Jules? Are *all* of your students lacking in energy and engagement?

Jules: Not all of them, as I think about it – in fact, only a few are seriously slacking. But somehow the whole tone of the class has shifted, and even the better students look disaffected.

Russell: Student faces grow predictably grumpy as the term proceeds. They want to see us as the enemy, themselves as victims of another round of tedious, compulsory education, their basic task as exerting the least amount of effort. I guess it's time to start collecting homework and grading it. That'll snap them out of their funk!

Jules: I'm not wholly comfortable with such a heavy-handed response.

Russell: Sometimes heavy-handedness is in the cards.

Jules: I wouldn't have pegged you for a Tarot reader, Russell! Doesn't such heavy-handedness simply reinforce the adversarial notion of teacher-as-enemy? To counter a lack of enthusiasm for learning with a more bureaucratic teaching style seems insulting to the strongest students, and it would motivate the others, if at all, in a manner precisely calculated to make them still more resentful.

Russell: You're still young and optimistic, Jules. You can't be nice to them as a reward for their intransigence. That will just give them more rope to hang you with. If the class begins to drag because few are involved, and they realize there's no immediate penalty for not preparing or participating, things just keep spiraling downward.

Jules: Yes, I've noticed.

Russell: But it gets worse. The awkward silences grow longer, suggesting that something has gone wrong with your teaching. And they will never blame themselves. Instead, they'll blame you, the institution, or the students who do participate.

Jules: Maybe so, Russell, but at what point do we begin to treat them as adults? Until we do, the most important lesson of college will be lost.

Alison: What lesson is that, Jules?

Jules: That real learning is an active, life-long, cooperative project of knowledge construction that requires great personal effort and motivation.

Russell: Look Jules, I thought we settled that over our last dinner at Alison's. The extreme skeptical notion that we construct the world for ourselves is a philosophical dead end.[3]

Jules: My radical constructivist days are largely behind me, thanks in part to you two. I'm now claiming nothing more than that it's hard to imagine how real learning could ever be imposed from the outside.

---

[3] See Johnson and Silliman, *Bridges to the World: A Dialogue on the Construction of Knowledge, Education, and Truth.*

Russell: I'm inclined to agree that no one learns anything really well until he or she wants to, Jules, but be realistic! If students don't want to get involved or do their work for whatever reason, then we've got no choice but to *make* them do it.

Alison: Are you suggesting that the end justifies the means, Russell? What kind of lesson is that?

Russell: I take your point, Alison, but teaching is not always sweetness and light. The least active, least motivated students probably won't be able to break free of bad habits by themselves and see what we're up to.

Alison: But shouldn't we help them understand our methods?

Russell: Good luck with that! Given a lifetime of compulsory schooling often marked by rigid top-down direction and manipulation, they will always be inclined to interpret your open, inviting style as some mistake or laziness on your part. And if they heard me say that, they might just withdraw further or become defensive – don't forget, you are the enemy!

Alison: Maybe in the minds of *some* students…

Russell: My bet is that you will capture the imaginations of only the very best. Most of the grumpiness will persist.

Alison: I feel your pain, Russell. Teaching is difficult, and even when we're at our best problems never stay solved for long. But Jules is right, not only about the inherent absurdity of coerced learning, but about the delicacy of the atmosphere in a classroom. A grumpy, adversarial attitude can be infectious. There has to be a better approach.

Jules: I think you're entirely right about what our students are mostly used to, Russell: old-fashioned talk-and-chalk lecturing, where the teacher's role is to be a kind of entertaining know-it-all, force-feeding students a steady diet of scripted data. I suppose I could conduct my classes that way – it might even make my life more predictable and relaxing. But I think it would be the wrong thing to do.

Russell: In my long experience, there is no real alternative. As distasteful or authoritarian as it may sound, you've got to admit that lecturing and giving objective examinations both work!

Jules: With all due respect for your many years in the classroom, Russell, I'm afraid it only *appears* to work. It gives the illusion of steady, predictable progress through some content or other, and makes students feel comfortable, even if they look grumpy – after all, it's the kind of schooling they've come to expect.

Russell: So our approach is fulfilling their expectations…

Jules: But the question whether it's any good or not, whether it succeeds in instilling in them a genuine love for learning, whether anything they internalize in this way lasts for more than a month – all of that is up for grabs. This is all too easy a method for teachers to adopt as well, since it conforms to their training and, as you suggest, it at least *seems* to meet students' expectations – even while it makes them even grumpier.

Alison: Yes, what becomes of the idea that learning occurs when students make a conscious choice to further their understanding and to do what is necessary to make that happen? It's not easy, it's never a passive affair, and it certainly isn't predicable or comfortable all of the time.

Russell: Okay, leading college students by the hand and taking charge may not be the most effective way to get them to perceive the power of self-directed learning. I see the irony there. But at least I know I'm getting something done! I can avoid all the awkward silences, grumpy looks, and silly questions you will get by doing things your way.

Jules: If genuine learning occurs, I can live with some confusion and the occasional silly question.

Russell: To each his own.

Jules: In my view, Russell, you're not really overcoming the strange grumpiness if you don't address it; the silly questions aren't going away, they're just getting buried in a flurry of activity followed by mindless student repetition. And the awkward moments of silence, which don't seem so awkward after a while, at least present a daily opportunity for someone to think, to get involved, to make a difference.

Russell: Now you seem to be talking yourself out of the concern we started with. Look: it's our job to get students working and thinking, whether they like it or not. They can grow up some other time, on someone else's watch. We won't get past chapter one if we have to worry about the ideological purity of our approach to learning!

Jules: Coverage of material as an end in itself may be the most stubborn ideology of all. Ignoring the affective or motivational deficits of our students simply exacerbates the grumpy syndrome.

Russell: Well, that's their problem, not ours. Right?

Alison: You're sounding a bit harsh and dogmatic today, Russell! Let's try to focus our attention on Jules' problem.

Russell: Maybe I just need another cup of coffee. But tell me this, what exactly do you think the problem is, Alison?

Alison: At root, it seems to me the question is whether or to what extent paternalism, or in gender-neutral terms that John Locke might appreciate, *parentalism*[4] is appropriate in educational contexts.

Problems of Paternalism

Jules: Well, my initial intuition is that paternalism has no place in higher education. Students are not our children, and we are not their parents.

Alison: We need not limit ourselves to the literal interpretation of the word. I think it's more about acting on behalf of others with or without their consent. Isn't that how philosophers use the term Russell?

Russell: Consent is key. Justifiable acts of paternalism set out to advance the interests of persons who would not otherwise effectively pursue those interests – or even recognize what they are – without outside help. If I *consent* to your direction, then we're only talking about "self-paternalism," which is even easier to justify. We do this all the time when we participate in framing laws that will constrain our future options.

Alison: So paternalists act for what they take to be the good of others...

Jules: But at the expense of the liberty of those others, at least in the short run.

---

4 In his *Second Treatise of Government*, Locke correctly anticipates later feminist observations of masculinist bias in prevailing terminology.

Russell: That's the problem with paternalism: "It is controversial because its end is benevolent, and its means coercive."[5]

Jules: So despite their good intentions, paternalists always do wrong.

Russell: Not so fast. It's *errantly* paternalistic only if the coercion is unjustified…

Jules: Can coercion ever really be justified? We're not talking about infants or young children. However immature they may seem at times, students in college classrooms are legal adults. The longer we treat them otherwise, the harder it will be for them to grow up and take charge of their lives. In fact, I pursued an advanced degree precisely so that I *could* teach adults, rather than children.

Alison: It's hard to argue with your point as an ideal principle, especially at the college level. But judging by what he said before, Russell seems to think it's unrealistic in practice, and I don't know yet what I think.

Russell: Like it or not – and it's pretty clear we don't -- most of our students are not equipped to make many of the most important choices about their learning or their lives. They need guidance, and considerable nudging.

Jules: "Nudging" is just another name for coercion.

Russell: Call it what you like, we all do it. I take it, Jules, that you assign specific readings, give detailed instructions for the various writing exercises your students must complete, and require that they do these things as a condition of completing your courses?

---

5 See, for example, Peter Suber's essay "Paternalism."

Jules: Of course I do! But this is an instance of what you call "self-paternalism." Students *elect* to take my courses, just as they elect to go to college in the first place. Since I make my expectations clear from the beginning, along with the consequences of ignoring them, I do not thereby patronize, but rather show respect for students.

Alison: What sort of thing *would* you consider errantly paternalistic, then?

Jules: Well, for one thing, I never call on my students unless they indicate their willingness to contribute to the discussion.

Alison: But you make participation an explicit expectation of the course?

Jules: Precisely.

Russell: How well does that work for you, generally speaking? If your classes are like mine, there is a very wide range of preparedness to contribute freely to class discussions. Those who jump right in get lots of practice, while those who are less sure of themselves, or not as quick on the draw, lose out unless I actively encourage them to speak their minds from time to time.

Jules: By 'actively encourage' I suppose you mean that you call on them.

Russell: I certainly do.

Jules: Surely there's some way to encourage the more reticent students to join in without such autocratic tactics?

Alison: Carefully designed small-group work, peer-editing, and collaborative exam-drafting, can sometimes embolden the quieter student to start speaking up in the larger discussion as well.

Jules: That's exactly the kind of thinking I'm looking for. I'm always happy to structure the class in ways that encourage involvement. But, on principle, I'm not comfortable asking students to speak who don't volunteer to do so. Calling on nonparticipating students simply infantilizes them. Adults, especially freshly minted ones, are entitled to make their own choices about when and how to engage in a conversation.

Russell: That principle sounds fine, but I don't think you or anyone else can live up to it. You require your students to join the conversation, yet you won't stoop to helping them do so, at least not directly. I have many students who identify themselves as 'shy,' as if shyness were a life sentence or a permanent medical condition. No doubt you've encountered these "shy rights activists."

Jules: Dozens of them. We certainly agree that self-justifying passivity is both common and lamentable. But what are we to do about it?

Russell: As I've said, we simply have to push them through it. I have yet to find an effective alternative.

Alison: Many students have spent their lives attempting, usually with very limited success, to learn passively. I confess that, like Russell, I sometimes draw them out by asking their opinions directly, and I can get very thoughtful contributions in response.

Jules: Sometimes, though surely not always.

Alison: Probably more often I fail, to be honest. But we have to keep trying.

Jules: Of course, but you and Russell seem willing to risk a high degree of embarrassment, and other sorts of distress, among these self-described shy students, for the relatively rare instances where it succeeds in drawing them out. And even when it works, have you really shown them that they can contribute fruitfully, or merely reinforced their expectation that they can wait until called upon?

Alison: That depends in part on the particular students, and whether my manner of drawing them out generates a sense of empowerment or its opposite. It also depends on how frequently I call on them, and whether I manage to convey that my doing so is transitional rather than a normal pattern. Like you, my desire and aim is that they come to need less prodding.

Jules: Do you indicate this by saying so, and discussing your pedagogical goals with them?

Alison: That is part of my procedure, yes, and I consider it very important. I always try to explain to students the pedagogical reasons for every element of the course design and procedure.

Russell: I'm guessing that this particular point is not one most of them are especially well equipped to absorb.

Alison: Once again, if I'm being honest, I would concede that in general you're right.

Jules: So you're not claiming to be uniquely *successful* at drawing the students out with your paternalistic procedure, even when you explain your methods to them?

Alison: Well, no. But here's another strategy. My students write and evaluate discussion questions in preparation for every reading, and I often go around the room and ask them all to read their questions to the class. This seems to me no more paternalistic than giving the assignment in the first place, and it neatly gets a range of issues on the table so I can guide the conversation where I think it needs to go – or focus on questions from those students I most want to draw in.

Jules: I'm much less uncomfortable with a procedure of this sort than I am with calling on students cold.

Russell: What do you mean, "cold?" As you say, they signed up for the course, and they have chosen to be students. Just as carpenters don't show up for work without their tools, students should be prepared to engage the material.

Alison: Russell has a point, Jules. By my own admission I am calling on all students, and to some extent manipulating the conversation to get them involved. I will ask a student to explain his or her question, for example, or invite other students to introduce related textual passages or ideas. Since I often use this to draw out the quieter types, I don't really see how this is any *less* paternalistic than what Russell suggests. Yet I also don't see that there is anything wrong with it.

Jules: In this procedure, at least, the focus is directly on the subject-matter, and the question is one the student has presumably spent some little time preparing, so the assault on the student's autonomy seems a little less acute.

Russell: Psychologically that may be true, and I can see that for just this reason it may be a more *effective* strategy, but I don't see at all how it is less *directive*. It's just a kinder and gentler way of *being* directive, so on principle I would expect you to reject it, Jules, for the same reason you decline to call on students.

Jules: Well, I can see that it's a *little* manipulative. Wouldn't you both think it better to have students who were active, curious, engaged, and at the same time sensitive to each other, so that the conversation would flow without such machinations on the part of the instructor?

Alison: You can only teach the students you've got, not the students you wish you had. The fact is I'd be happy if they were simply curious, since I think the rest would follow with only a little guidance. But given what we're faced with, we must seek out ways to move students toward their own intellectual and emotional maturity.

Jules: Very Rumsfeldian,[6] Alison, but it seems to me the only way for them to *become* the students, and persons, that they need and ought to be is to treat them, prospectively, *as though* that is who they already are.

Russell: I see the sense of your idealism, Jules. But teachers face a paradox: we are working with nominally autonomous persons, yet our job description demands that we *change* them – instill some skill, disposition, or understanding that they lack – in Alison's construction, help them become more autonomous.

Jules: I get that it's our job to make students into different people, in some sense, but why does this give us license to be paternalistic?

Russell: If they like themselves the way they are, and most do, they will find the change painful or disruptive, and naturally resist it. We may not shirk our obligation to insist, one way or another, that they learn despite this natural resistance. I take it you would not treat eight-year-olds as though they were adults so as to encourage them to grow up…?

Jules: No, of course not. A considerable measure of paternalism is entirely age-appropriate for small children – and by and large, that's what parents are for.

Alison: Surely human autonomy is developmental, and a matter of degree, so that even when elementary teachers relate to children *in*

---

6 In 2004, responding to concerns about sending ill-equipped soldiers to fight in Iraq, President George W. Bush's Secretary of Defense, Donald Rumsfeld said, "You go to war with the army you have, not the army you might want or wish to have."

loco parentis, they are hoping to edge them toward a more mature relationship with their teachers and others?

Russell: Exactly, and to that extent teachers should also, at the same time, treat children as adults – in incremental, age-appropriate ways. Without that, most of them would probably end up in a sort of eternal adolescence, forever dependent emotionally, intellectually, and materially on others, while at the same time defiant and defensive about the independence they crave but can't actualize.

Jules: I'm glad you see it this way, Russell, since the Gradgrindian[7] procedure you have been recommending for teaching college students is likely to have the very effect you describe. An awful lot of people seem in fact to be extending their adolescences for several decades, so perhaps you have hit on a trenchant critique of our educational systems at every level. But your prescription reinforces it!

Russell: These are indeed hard times, and we three alone will not solve the culture's problems. Until they are solved, we must do our best with the students we've got, in Alison's memorable phrase.

Jules: I cannot accept this fatalism. We have to find a way to honor and foster our students' autonomy fully, and thus coddle them no further, both for their own sakes and as our professional obligation. They are no longer eight years old, after all.

Alison: But Jules, if you're right that they have been coddled too long, many of them may actually *be* eight in an important sense, or not much older. This sounds harsh, and I don't mean to insult anyone, but it's clear that the kind of maturity required for

---

7 Thomas Gradgrind is the bullying, authoritarian schoolmaster in Charles Dickens's *Hard Times*.

intellectual work is in short supply in the culture at large, not least among college students.

Russell: I'm afraid that's true.

Alison: And it won't do to wish it away. I can agree with you that an educational system that was better designed and better run than ours would treat promoting various types of maturity as a defining goal, progressively strengthening autonomy at every stage. The point of education would *not* be primarily to produce skilled or compliant workers, but rather imaginative, curious, poised, energetic, and self-directed persons.

Russell: I detect a note of cynicism about whether you think that is our educational system's aim.

Alison: Your detection is acute. Look, so long as our students seem to require a certain degree of paternalistic guidance, why not simply provide it, along with a general push toward greater autonomy?

Jules: But Alison, that's fatalistic, and counterproductive as well. It's just wrong to compromise our training and commitment as professional educators merely because the schools, the parents, and the culture aren't doing their respective jobs, or even understand fully what their jobs are. Worse, it simply doesn't work. Treat students like infants, and infants they will remain. Not to mention the dumbing-down effect this has on those students who *are* prepared to do college work.

Alison: Jules, you over-interpret my words. I'm not advocating fatalism or moral compromise, but intelligent accommodation to our actual situation. Let me propose a counter-principle to your blanket rejection of paternalism:

> *We should wield our quasi-paternal authority always and only in ways that progressively foster our students' autonomy.*

And the first corollary to the application of this principle is that we never neglect the interests of those students who, as you say, really *are* prepared to learn.

Jules: I can see that your principle attempts to make up for some of the lost opportunities in our students' earlier educational experiences, but I don't yet see how, while letting this paternal camel's nose under the tent, you will succeed in supporting the good students.

Alison: We can do so, in the first instance, by enlisting them in the process of bringing the others along, and in ways that are educationally useful to themselves.

Russell: I'm all ears, Alison.

Alison: From your own experience I'm sure you'll agree that we seldom understand something unless we can explain it to someone else, and we often imagine we understand it, only to discover in conversation that we are muddled or unclear about it.

Jules: That is a common phenomenon, yes.

Alison: It follows that a well crafted exercise, putting the best students in a position of articulating what they've learned in language that the struggling students can understand, benefits everyone.

Jules: Of course, though it's a delicate thing to pull off. I don't quite see how this instantiates your "progressive paternalism" axiom, however.

Alison: It doesn't, particularly. It's just an example of how it's not necessarily impossible to bring marginal students along without undermining the learning of the more mature ones.

Russell: It serves that purpose well enough. But I'm curious what mild paternalism would actually look like in the classroom.

Grounding Paternalism

Alison: I'm curious, too, but maybe it would help to coin a descriptive name for what we're proposing. How about "grounded paternalism," where directive teaching is justified only to the extent that it both honors the dignity of students as persons and encourages the growth of that autonomy?

Jules: Back up one step first; I don't yet accept that we should admit paternalism *at all*, grounded or not, if it's autonomy that we really value!

Russell: I think I can help out there. Some people associate full autonomy with radical individualism, as though a person could ever be entirely independent of others. But we're a social species, and there's no opting out – language itself, the core medium through which we express our very individuality, is a cultural inheritance millennia in the making. In this and other ways, *any* degree of autonomous personhood is always actually a *social* accomplishment.

Alison: That's an important reminder, Russell, and if we hope to avoid the libertarian fallacy of reductive individualism, we must ensure that the autonomy we help to actualize in our students involves socially shared purposes and understandings. We have no license for arbitrary authority; we are guides. But a guide must sometimes be a director.

Jules: I'm no radical libertarian, and I follow your reasoning, but your image sounds just a little conformist to me.

Alison: I certainly don't intend it that way, Jules. Note my pointed use of plural nouns – shared purpose*s* and understanding*s*. My point is that when we stop fantasizing about being above society, politics, or whatever, we can begin to think about institutions of learning as incubators of socially grounded creativity, *not* conformity factories. If we lean on students, when necessary, in this socially grounded, empowering spirit, the paradox dissolves.

Russell: "Dissolves" might be too strong. After all, a genuine paradox is not merely a puzzle to be solved, so much as a labyrinth that we endlessly negotiate.

Jules: Nevertheless, Alison's principle seems worth a try, as it relieves some of the cognitive dissonance of the paradox. To the extent that grounded paternalism is successful, it would progressively undermine the need for itself, so although it employs methods I find distasteful, at least it actively aims eventually to transcend them.

Russell: It is appealing on those grounds. I also see some parallels in Alison's idea of grounded paternalism with the concept of a "nudge" in public policy, which some people advocate as a way to make governance more effective and less intrusive.

Jules: How is that supposed to work?

Russell: Well, it begins with the intuition that legislation is most effective, and least authoritarian, when it mainly *educates* rather than *threatens*. If you want students to choose healthier foods in a cafeteria, simply place the healthy foods at eye level and make the others slightly less visible. That way we can support people's best impulses through thoughtful "choice architecture" without diminishing the range of choice – hence the strange-sounding notion of "libertarian paternalism."[8]

Alison: That does have a paradoxical ring. And you think this might be a model for some of our issues in classrooms, not just in the cafeteria?

Russell: I sure do; the cafeteria is just an example that's actually been tested. We frame the choice architecture in the classroom constantly, and in myriad ways – by giving a list of possible paper topics, or how we arrange the seating in the room, and so forth. Part of the craft of teaching is to become sensitive to how small things like this affect the students' frame of mind and disposition to engage.

Jules: I can't disagree with you that we do these things, Russell, and even that our teaching improves when we are alert to them. I'm not entirely comfortable, however, with the suggestion that the autonomy we're seeking to foster in our students is essentially a matter of consumer choice.

Alison: Jules has a point there, Russell. When I speak of autonomy I'm thinking of the term's etymology: a person capable of self-governance, remembering Kant's definition of freedom as "action in accordance with a law you give yourself."[9] I'm not opposed to your "nudge" idea, either in the crafting of law or the framing of a lesson plan, but I think teachers should aspire to do more than help their students become more effective shoppers.

Russell: Your concern is legitimate, but it exaggerates my sense of the value of a nudge. I don't think maximizing choice is the same as autonomy, or even an end in itself, but rather a principled means of supporting students' growth. It is at least one measure

---
8 See Richard H. Thaler and Cass R. Sunstein, *Nudge*.
9 Immanuel Kant, *Foundations of the Metaphysics of Morals*.

of the bounds I place on my paternalism, if I have not greatly or arbitrarily circumscribed the choices open to my students.

Jules: I accept that gloss on your suggestion, and as I said I'm otherwise intrigued. What then about old-fashioned chalk-and-talk lecturing? Wouldn't you say that this ancient classroom style is the sort of thing that limits the range of students' choices, and undermines autonomy?

Russell: Well, that's a question that cuts close to the bone, as I am one of those dinosaurs who still gives my students a rousing lecture from time to time. I have to say that really great lectures are part of what drew me into academia in the first place, and I still think that done well – and used sparingly – they can be dynamic and inspiring educational experiences.

Jules: For the students, or for yourself?

Russell: I'm not ashamed to admit that I sometimes spontaneously discover new ideas and connections while waxing eloquent for my classes, but I don't think that's inconsistent with students being informed and inspired by it as well.

Alison: No need to put Russell on the defensive, Jules. I imagine you've enjoyed a few brilliant lectures yourself at one time or another, and he does concede that its uses are limited.

Jules: I don't think lecturing is categorically bad teaching, but it is suspect. Absent the give-and-take of classroom dialogue, it can be very difficult to determine whether you are supporting students in their intellectual maturity, or furthering their infantilization. Are you teaching, or merely talking?

Russell: Your suspicion is well founded, Jules, which is why I not only use the form sparingly, but also have writing assignments designed to help the students process the information. And, *loco parentis* that I am, I also check whether they have absorbed my tirades in intelligent ways.

Jules: That goes some way toward limiting the damage, I suppose, but I still think a straight lecture is the very embodiment of the wrong sort of paternalism. I can hear Gradgrind hyperventilating now, pounding home the definition of a horse: *"Graminiverous Ruminating Quadruped!"*

Alison: I studied with Russell some years ago, and he's no Dickensian parody.

Russell: Thank you, Alison. Maybe we should take up the merits of lectures further at some point. I've got a lot more to say on the subject.

Jules: I'll bet you do!

Interlude

Jules Randolph Govier

I cannot remember ever wanting to be anything but a teacher. School for me, from kindergarten forward, was primarily an opportunity to observe and think about my teachers' methods. Why I fixed so young and intensely upon this interest I have no idea. That my mother was a teacher by profession and character seems insufficient. I love her very much, but I don't think I aspired to *be* her. Whatever its source, on the whole this focus made me a pretty effective student. Maybe paying attention at several levels at once aided my comprehension of the subject matter and the discipline itself. The teachers I thought most effective were almost always those with a flair for imaginative empathy – they understood why something was hard for a student to understand, and could quickly improvise a story, an example, or an analogy that would bring it to life for that very child. I longed for little else in life but to acquire such a talent.

My father I admired enormously, not for his own central passion, which was architecture, but for his role as an Engineering professor at New York University. Though his students were not his main focus, I could see how much they loved and respected him for his brilliance and patience.

So, not surprisingly, I was pretty shocked that most students in my education courses seemed to have stumbled into the field, as if they pursued teaching because they were at a loss for a better idea. By contrast, I experienced the prospect of teaching like a crystal clear vocation, practically audible, as though the world and my nature were literally calling me to do it. I know this is an old-fashioned and excessively romantic notion, and my family was anything but religious, but that's the way I felt, and I still feel that way today.

Chapter Two

Between Teaching and Learning

What is the nature of knowing or understanding in a pedagogical context? That is, what does it mean to learn or to teach something? And failing a direct answer to that question, might we find a useful image for thinking about the process? Our goal is to find a bridge from teaching to learning, since the two are evidently independent of one another: people often learn without being taught, and far too much teaching results in little or no learning.

What is Learning?

Alison: I think we might be getting ahead of ourselves. How can we settle anything important about how to teach if we don't understand a little more deeply what learning is?

Russell: I think it's pretty clear that learning is the assimilation of new knowledge.

Jules: That's difficult to disagree with, Russell, but hardly informative, since all of its key terms are problematic.

Russell: Of course they are, Jules. I only offer it as a place to start. Take 'knowledge,' for instance. We don't have to rehearse the history of epistemology to speak in practical terms of what it means to know. I know calculus, you know French, and the three of us know each other quite well.

Jules: Those are three rather distinct species of knowing, I would say.

Alison: They certainly are. I also know how to play the piano, which might be yet another variety.

Russell: But let's focus on what all of our examples have in common. Each is something the knower acquires through his or her volition.

Alison: That's true of my continuing desire to play the piano and your advanced mathematical abilities. But there is less deliberate choice involved in speaking French, especially if you learned it as a child among native French-speakers.

Jules: Which, as it happens, I did.

Alison: And I will concede that our mutual acquaintance is something I chose, and gladly, but it might have been otherwise – often people find themselves thrown together, and they get to know each other whether they want to or not. Plus, if volition is critical to learning and knowing, compulsory schooling seems more than just a little awkward.

Russell: Awkward isn't the word for it; compulsory schooling is a genuine conundrum, if not an outright oxymoron. I suspect it is only effective because the natural impulse to learn is so deep in some people that it's very hard to stop them from learning, no matter how badly you mistreat them.

Jules: So it seems that volition is *not* a prominent feature of all knowledge acquisition, after all.

Russell: I accept that it is more prominent in some cases than others, but I would insist that it's present to some degree in the acquisition of all knowledge. And that's simply because I think internal motives and dispositions – curiosity, caring, manipulating or categorizing objects in the world – undergird all of our deliberate activities, both cognitive and bodily.

Jules: Okay, let's assume that all knowledge is to some degree purposeful. I'm inclined to add that knowledge is not so much something we *have* as something we can *do*. In this light, the acquiring of it involves not only volition but also a fair degree of practice or exploration.

Learning Something as Knowing How

Russell: You might be onto something, Jules. There's an old distinction between *knowing that* and *knowing how* that we should probably set aside if we are to think of learning in general in these terms.[10]

Alison: But that distinction seems to me to mark a meaningful difference. Some kinds of abilities are less cognitive or discursive than they are emotive, visceral, or muscular, like certain moments when I'm improvising at the piano. Moreover, I can know a lot *about* something – tennis, for example – without really being able to do it well.

Jules: True enough. *knowing that* tennis is played a particular way is distinct from *knowing how* to play it. It is useful, however, to think of all knowledge, even what seem purely cognitive abilities, as *things we can do*. In this respect, learning the rules of tennis is very much like learning how to play tennis. After all, *all* sorts of abilities involve the coordination of both muscles and neurons, albeit to varying degrees.

---

10 Namely, propositional *versus* practical knowledge.

Alison: And I suppose my knowledge of tennis isn't very profound or well rounded if I can't also perform it. This sounds like a paraphrase of Kant: comprehension without practice is empty, practice without comprehension is blind.[11]

Russell: That's a clever reading of Kant, Alison. In thus collapsing 'knowing that' into 'knowing how,' we are not denying that it's possible to learn in shallow or merely verbal ways. Much of conventional schooling consists in empty learning like this, thin as newsprint and ephemeral as the next exam. We're arguing, rather, that the learning we should seek to foment is of a much more profound and integral character.

Jules: I like it. Let's accept this account of learning provisionally, then, as *things we can do, the acquisition of which involves some degree of volition*. One thing I like about this way of thinking is that it emphasizes that learning a subject is not merely accumulating facts, or even just acquiring a vocabulary for speaking about them.

Russell: Although we certainly need to accumulate facts and vocabulary in order to learn a subject.

Jules: Agreed. But those things are just the precursors to any well developed ability. Mastery of a discipline is not confined to gathering facts and words. It involves entering viscerally and rigorously into a particular universe of discourse. And each of these discursive worlds constitutes a specific way of seeing, feeling, and thinking. Only from inside such a framework can we meaningfully engage that activity, be it philosophy or biology, just as we can't play tennis well until we have internalized the rules.

Alison: I can see that conceiving of each discipline as analogous to a game – like tennis, or perhaps a more team-oriented sport –

---

11 Mirroring Kant's observation that "Thoughts without content are empty, intuitions without concepts are blind," *Critique of Pure Reason*, p. 93.

enriches and clarifies our provisional claim of what it is to learn. We wouldn't want to push the sports analogy too far, though. Healthy intellectual disciplines do not operate on fixed rules, a win-or-lose mentality, or wall themselves off from other ways of seeing.

Russell: I agree, Alison. Jules's description of a "universe of discourse" is fine as far as it goes, and as a professional I appreciate the in-group conversations I can have with a community of similarly trained philosophers. But there has to be a dynamic conversation with those outside that group as well, to keep the profession alive and honest. Teaching is one way to stay in touch with thinking outside your specialty, and as I have become more attuned to that practice – thanks in part to your prompting, Alison — I think I have also become a better philosopher as well.

Alison: You're both right. A field of study at once embodies a unique and distinguishable approach to looking at the world, and a mere page in the book of learning, of limited use unless informed by the rest of the pages. Something rather strange and interesting follows from what we've said, though. If learning is always the intentional acquisition of an ability, it's hard to see how teaching in the conventional sense is possible at all.

Russell: Why do you say that?

Jules: I think I see what she means. There's a pretty wide gap between telling someone how to do something and that person intending to acquire – let alone succeed in acquiring – that ability. There's room for a bit of coaching perhaps, a pointer, some encouragement or the demonstration of a particular technique, but no actual *teaching* as traditionally conceived.

Alison: As we discussed earlier, I've never really believed that the old-fashioned didactic style had much to do with teaching anyway. It seems to me that teachers from Plato to Dewey have effectively debunked the naïve notion that a teacher could transfer intact packets of information directly to students.

Jules: Though the notion of teaching as simple information transfer from expert to novice persists with a vengeance, for all that.

Russell: So it does, and not without some justification. Since this keeps coming up, I'd like to try to defend the traditional lecture format as consistent with the view of learning as consciously intending to, and then acquiring, the ability to do something. I know the two of you are doubtful of its value, but I'm not ready to give up on it. I agree that it's not all there is to teaching, but it has its place.

Alison: How will you make your defense, Russell?

Russell: With your permission, I will give a short lecture on the matter. How else?

Jules: If you must. I'll try my best to learn something, despite the obvious pedagogical obstacles.

Russell: Very funny, Jules. Let me make four main points followed by a qualification, and then sum up.

Lecture on Lectures

- In the first place, a lecturer who is deeply immersed in the subject can, even when speaking extemporaneously as I am now, uncover and elucidate valuable insights that it might take students a very long time to discover on their own. If students are curious and attentive, a lecture can thus serve as an opportunity to advance their learning quite efficiently. I readily concede that if they lack either curiosity or attentiveness, students will acquire little from a lecture, but we can fairly say the same for reading, practicing a skill, or having a discussion. Curiosity and attention are propaedeutic[12] in any case, as elements of applied volition that are desiderata of any serious learning.

- In the second place, the format of a lecture gives the teacher space to lay out an organizational structure for the material – to provide the students with a sort of mental coat-hanger for information related to the topic. If the hanger is sturdy and has well ordered brackets, students may acquire a powerful cognitive tool for the discipline even if most of the details happen to slide temporarily to the floor. Or, more usually, get garbled in their notes. Not incidentally, a lecture is a wonderful medium for stretching a metaphor a little too far, as well as indulging in a bit of light relief.

- Thirdly, a well crafted lecture, like a really good story, has affective as well as cognitive benefits. Eloquence has its own, compelling aesthetic, and an effective speaker can be a real inspiration for students. It can model enthusiasm for learning and systematic reasoning from disparate sources of evidence, and stimulate in students the aspiration to become knowledgeable themselves. For many of us the life of the mind is, or should be, one of mystery, excitement, and surprise – essential elements often missing from the academy today. We might do well to revive the much-maligned notion of lecturer-as-entertainer, given widespread stereotypes in the culture about the dryness and irrelevance of scholarship.

---

12 Etymologically propaedeutic is from the Greek verb for education, *paidein* (literally to lead a child). Something propaedeutic is a thing we must learn or accept before we can proceed.

- Finally, I think occasional, well crafted lectures are a fine antidote to the lamentable habit of some professors to fetishize uninformed student opinions. Important as I take class discussion to be, it can at times devolve into random, disconnected comments from unprepared students who have learned that they can earn praise simply by shooting wildly from the hip. A lecture that develops a systematic argument for some definite claim both models organized, scholarly thinking and lays a solid foundation for meaningful, informed questions and discussion.

I do not, of course, claim that the lecture method alone is sufficient for serious learning. I insist only that it has a legitimate place in the pantheon of teaching techniques. And that's because it really is not possible to download information, much less comprehension, into students' heads directly. They must hear and see, then read and articulate for themselves, and repeat this pattern frequently in order to learn any important subject. I would even go so far as to concede that the decline of the lecture format in contemporary colleges and universities is partly justified, given changes in the culture affecting the preparedness of students to profit by it. This has justly raised the bar for lecturers to craft their comments well, pitch them advisedly, and vary their teaching methods, so as to ensure they are in fact teaching, not merely talking.

To summarize, lecture can be efficient, organizationally and informationally useful, entertaining, and inspiring. We should be careful not to overuse it, but to jettison it altogether would be like throwing the cat out with the kitty litter.

Jules: I have to say, Russell, that was not bad. Clear, crisp, and mercifully brief, though a couple of those sentences were long enough to dry laundry.

Russell: Compliment accepted, Jules, however back-handed. I would of course tighten up the style and reparse the vocabulary if I were actually going to deliver it to students.

Alison: I'm impressed, too, Russell. I'm not sure we're really in disagreement, though. The claim I was rejecting was the old-fashioned idea that teachers can deliver knowledge wholesale into the minds of students. Your description – and fine example – of a good lecture makes no pretence to mechanical data-transfer.

Russell: Thanks. There is no question that intrinsic motivation and focused volition, the prerequisites for what educators call 'active learning,' is indispensable. Lecture can only supplement the process at strategic moments, though it can do so beautifully in the hands of a master teacher in creative command of the material.

Jules: This is useful – and I grudgingly concede that I may have been underestimating the value of lecture – but I think maybe we've gotten a bit off-track. We were trying to pin down what learning is, and Alison questioned our definition of it as the partially voluntary acquisition of abilities, on the grounds that it didn't leave much scope for teaching as conventionally understood.

Alison: In fact, I rather like our current formulation of learning, or coming to know something. I was simply wondering about its implications for teachers. Russell's defense of lecturing does not claim that even a brilliant lecturer can download data to student brains, and he shows how a teacher can do more than offer sporadic tips or coaching.

Jules: How, exactly?

Alison: By providing both a certain kind of intellectual and even personal inspiration, as well as simplifying frameworks for understanding – mental coat hangers, you called them, Russell?

Russell: Yes.

Alison: With the use of pedagogical tools like scientific theories, metaphors, analogies, methods, and conventions, teachers can aid both comprehension and memory in students, and lay a foundation for more active engagement afterward.

Jules: Okay, I see that this is possible, but it also seems dangerous. Models, metanarratives, and conceptual frameworks are always, as Russell says, simplifications, and they can thereby do as much to obscure a subject as illuminate it. The danger lies in their very simplicity, for it makes it too easy to accept a cramped, conventional view of something.[13]

Russell: Once again, Jules, we do not disagree as much as you think we do. A conceptual framework is a learning tool, not a straightjacket, and the teacher must regularly remind students that there will always be anomalous details and complexities that it does not capture. Pointing out that there are legitimate alternative models for organizing the same data is also helpful. I will add this salutary qualifier to my notes, in case I ever have occasion to give the lecture again.

Alison: And it is worth reminding students, perhaps, that constructing new and better conceptual frameworks is a crucial part of their task as learners – that models are merely tools we must use judiciously and regularly re-design, just as we re-draw a map after visiting the territory.

Jules: I wonder how many teachers are that frank with their students about the models they present? But even if we accept this

---

13 The Nobel laureate plant geneticist Barbara McClintock famously hated models, which she compared to cartoons or caricatures, concerned that they block both observation and original thought (see Evelyn Fox Keller, *A Feeling for the Organism*). In this she was perhaps in a minority among important scientists, but scarcely alone.

narrative of learning, I don't think we've yet explained what the *process* of learning is.

Russell: Well, it *is* a process, and a fairly complex one. Acknowledging that is a start, and I agree with you that there is more to it than we've found so far.

Consuming Learning

Alison: Here's a thought. If you're right about volition, Russell, and the acquisition of the ability to do something new, we might say that learning is *a process of taking something into yourself and making it a part of you*. This internalizes the element of volition, I think, and is metaphorically somatic enough to include the insight about ability as well.

Jules: By that way of framing it you seem to be suggesting that *eating* is a type of learning!

Russell: …and that compulsory schooling is a bit like inserting a feeding tube into a prisoner on a hunger strike. Neither victim gets much of value, though they can't help but absorb something eventually, even if at considerable cost to their autonomy.

Alison: Well, I didn't mean it quite so literally, but I like the digestion analogy. I'm sure you'll remind us, Russell, that the seventeenth century philosopher John Locke employs the process of eating and digesting to illustrate his account of natural property acquisition.[14] Perhaps it could be a useful image for acquiring knowledge as well as rightful possessions.

---

14 John Locke, *Two Treatises of Government*, II, 5, sect. 28. Locke describes a process of gathering, cooking, eating, and digesting as a model of our entitlement to those natural objects in which we invest ourselves in meeting our needs. Although this may not succeed in justifying private property, it nonetheless presents a fairly realistic psychological description of how we come to *feel a sense* of ownership in things.

Jules: That's a pretty interesting idea, Alison, that when you learn something in some sense you make it your own. Teachers often say how important it is that students take ownership of the material and the learning process, and the image suggests that neither you nor the thing you learn stay entirely the same.[15]

Russell: Let's give Locke's analogy some thought, using digestion as a metaphor for the process of acquiring and "taking ownership" of emotional and cognitive abilities.

Alison: At first blush, I think digestion could be a useful way to think about Piaget's learning cycle.

Russell: Help me out, you two. I'm not familiar with Piaget.

Jules: I don't mean to offend you personally, Russell, but I have to say it is pretty astonishing the things one can fail to know about pedagogy and still be a college professor.

Russell: No offense taken. I'm as appalled as anyone about the lacunae in my own training, and I struggled for many years under the delusion that effective teaching was an automatic by-product of knowing my subject well. It's one of many reasons I'm grateful for these talks of ours.

Alison: The idea of the learning cycle is that we start with some concrete experience, reflect on it to generate general hypotheses or schemas, and test these actively by seeking out further concrete

---

15 Analogies between eating and learning have a pedigree: "…education is not a process of packing articles in a trunk. Such a simile is entirely inapplicable. It is, of course, a process completely of its own particular genus. It's nearest analogue is the assimilation of food by a living organism: and we all know how necessary to health is palatable food under suitable conditions. When you have put your boots in a trunk they will stay there until you take them out again; but this is not at all the case if you feed a child with the wrong food." A.N. Whitehead, *The Aims of Education*, p. 33.

experience. By repeating this cycle, we absorb and eventually retain some understanding of whatever it is we're learning.[16]

Jules: There's even some surprising new evidence that our brains themselves are structured this way, and perform the learning cycle naturally from infancy.[17]

Alison: I don't see why that should surprise anyone, though I suppose it is independent confirmation that teachers *discovered* the cycle, and didn't just make it up.

Russell: This notion of a learning cycle would help explain my observation that young people often learn even when their schooling works against them doing so.

Jules: Yes, it would.

Alison: The reason I think digestion is a helpful image for the learning cycle is that through this sort of intimate engagement with some subject matter, we absorb it into ourselves. The process and the nature of the material – that is, our ability to do something new – change us.

Jules: If you're right, Alison, this would be an argument for maximizing volition, conscious choice, in seeking to learn. If we are what we eat, and become what we learn, we'll want to be careful about what we take in.

Alison: We put food in our mouths, process it in various mechanical and biochemical ways, and eventually absorb it into our bodies.

---

16 The psychologist Jean Piaget does not describe a "learning cycle" in so many words, but several educational theorists have done so based on his theories of cognitive reasoning and development. This simplified version derives from D.A. Kolb's *Experiential Learning*.
17 See Alison Gopnik, *The Philosophical Baby*, and James Zull, *The Art of Changing the Brain*.

Like learning, eating is an active process, and a collaborative one as well – we couldn't do it without those two or three trillion microbes in our digestive tracts, not to mention the social and economic networks that grow and deliver our food to us.

Jules: That's true, Alison, and with my background in biology I should have thought of it. Let me extend the metaphor. We digest what we learn by ruminating: moving back and forth between the theoretical and the practical. And, as you say, we change in the process. But the digestion metaphor would suggest that the subject matter is transformed as well…

Alison: It's clear that the learner changes – the point of learning is to become different – which is in part why it's often emotionally difficult, as Russell says. I'm not sure the metaphor works so well when it comes to the *objects* of learning.

Jules: Emboldened by seeming to be in agreement with Russell on this, let me see if I can make it out.

Russell: Okay, Jules, you have the floor.

Between Knower and Known

Jules: Presumably, Alison, you agree that your learning a new piece of music. A Mozart sonata, for example, does not merely replicate the score.

Alison: Well, yes. I can seldom do justice to a really great composition, so when I learn a new piece, the music generally suffers.

Jules: Self-deprecation aside – and I've heard you play beautifully – you accept the principle that each performance of a piece of music is a new interpretation of it. The score does not change, perhaps, but the music does.

Russell: I think you're right, Jules, that understood as a living, cultural artifact, even music that is well known and fully codified changes as musicians perform it, audiences hear it, and the qualities of their ears and instruments take shape and evolve. The change is not very much like what happens to an apple when you digest it, though.

Alison: We might be stretching our metaphor to the breaking point...

Jules: And yet, when a masterful performance of a piece really clicks, it can work a kind of transformative magic on all concerned.

Alison: Yes, I see that, and it's even clearer in the case of jazz, a genre rooted in relatively spontaneous improvisation and creative, often daring and unexpected communication between musicians, their audiences, and a variety of musical traditions.

Jules: I can also see how, by extension of this principle, speaking a language has a subtle effect on that language, just as no two tennis players embody the principles of the game in quite the same way. In this fashion the character of the game changes over time, though its constitutive rules may not.

Alison: But I'm having a little harder time accepting that my learning something fixed and objective, say arithmetic or the ancient Greek alphabet, has any effect at all on those codified objects. I don't think my learning the multiplication table affects it in the least.

Jules: Notice, however, that all the other examples we've mentioned illustrate varying *degrees* of responsiveness of the object to being learned. We could make a scale from highly elastic to relatively rigid, and locate on it all possible objects of understanding.

Russell: Presumably what we would find if we charted the variables is that the durability of a subject matter in response to learning will vary with certain features – things like its function in our lives, its degree of abstractness, size and antiquity, or the number of people who learn it. Make up your own language with a few friends, and learning a single new word by itself revolutionizes your communicative medium; learn Mandarin and your influence will be very slight, though still real.

Alison: Yes, perhaps, but I don't quite see how the periodic table of elements or Mount Everest are going anywhere just because I get to know them.

Jules: These sorts of things are very near the south end of our scale, of course, but for the reasons we've given, it's clear they are not off it altogether.

Alison: I guess I can see that. I'm intrigued by this line of thought because, if you're right about the transformation both of ourselves and what we learn in the learning process, it reinforces my intuition that learning involves the *active construction of knowledge*.

Constructivist Realism[18]

Russell: Careful! We wouldn't want to slip back into some radically incoherent notion of constructivism!

Alison: No fear of that. In my view learners' active construction of understanding is wholly consistent with the existence and

---

[18] The terminology in this section comes from Johnson and Silliman's *Bridges to the World*, especially the conclusions Alison draws in her letter to Jules that stands as that book's Epilogue.

(mediated) accessibility of the external world. I do insist, however, that our efforts to know things are filtered through the conceptual frameworks we construct for ourselves. To employ the sort of clunky neologisms so common in contemporary educational theory, the best name for my view would be "Constructivist Realism."

Russell: We've spoken of this idea extensively before, Alison, but maybe Jules would profit from an amplification of what you mean by it.

Alison: Is that a coy way of saying you'd like me to clarify it for you, Russell?

Russell: Well, I admit I am still a little muddled about how your view, as a theory of education, really differs from the fallible version of realism that I have so often defended myself.

Jules: Russell speaks for both of us this time, Alison, in hoping you will expound a little on this theory.

Alison: So now you're asking *me* to give a lecture! Am I the only one to see some irony in that request coming from you, Jules?

Jules: I'm not suggesting anything formal. Just briefly summarize your present view and your reasoning for it. My own grasp of these complexities is a little shaky and, as you know, I cut my theoretical teeth in graduate school on a heavy dose of radical constructivism, so memory tends to falter.

Alison: I love my intellectual friends, but you can be so demanding! Okay, if I must, a quick summary:

So-called Radical Constructivism[19] presents itself as a theory of knowing, hence of learning, that makes no reference, direct or indirect, to anything outside the knower. Knowledge, on its view, and the world itself as each of us knows it, must be wholly constructed by each knowing self. I won't go into the many ways this theory iterates and even amplifies the errors of radical skepticism and subjective relativism. In accordance with my affirming nature, I will instead seek for some crumbs of sense in its moldy loaf.

First, it is true – and useful for teachers to remember – that students always confront new information in relation to their own prior experience and the conceptual frameworks they have themselves built in order to make sense of that experience. Thus, although it is silly to think we have no perceptual or conceptual access to the outside world, it would be equally silly to assume that our access to it is direct, unmediated, infallible, or requires no interpretation. There are several practical consequences of taking this realization seriously.

- Most teachers observe that students learn best when subject matter connects to matters already familiar to them.

- Students need more than data to memorize. With well crafted tools for applying and thinking about what they learn, they comprehend and retain much better. I think you had this in mind, Russell, when you spoke a little while ago about mental coat-hangers, and of course the learning cycle embodies it.

- There are various legitimate interpretations of experience, so we need to cultivate empathy and patience with

---

19 Ernst von Glasersfeld was founder of the educational theory and movement of radical constructivism. See, for example, "An Introduction to Radical Constructivism."

students, and take care not to define intelligence narrowly. Cognitive skills that are easy to test are not necessarily the most important ones. I take this to be a core insight behind Gardner's notion of multiple intelligences, and though educators have sometimes exaggerated or abused this theory, I think it is basically sound.[20]

There is a useful sense in which we do in fact – as a community rather than as individuals – construct useful sub-worlds in order to focus on specific questions. You were just now calling these "universes of discourse," Jules, which are specific ways of seeing, feeling, thinking, and speaking about the world. I think we have already done some justice to both the power and the danger of constructions like these.

To answer your question, Russell, I find compelling your insistence that our veridical access to reality – with the possible exception of the basic, indubitable truths of logic and other axiomatic systems – is always fallible, always subject to correction and revision. Because we must exercise authority, arrogance is an occupational hazard for teachers, a kind of intellectual black lung disease, so you can't remind us too often that what we think we know is incomplete and correctible.

Russell: Thank you, Alison. For someone who claims not to be capable of lecturing, that was really impressive. Let me push you on your last point, however. You haven't yet completely answered my question about how what I call *fallible realism* differs in substance from what you call *constructivist realism*.

---

[20] See Howard Gardner's *Multiple Intelligences*. One way to misread the theory is to demand that it demonstrate its distinctions, or the precise number of distinct intelligences, with mathematical precision and clinical rigor. This is reductively to treat students and the complex process of intelligence as though they were simple machines. Testing and teaching for individual "learning styles" sometimes goes to the other extreme, where educators treat such differences as fixed and immutable facts about students.

Alison: The difference may primarily be a matter of emphasis. I agree with you that fallibility is a robust fact about human understanding, but I also find the notion of knowledge construction opens us to some specific pedagogical applications, such as those I just mentioned. In conversation with Jules, I have come to take very seriously the process by which we make sense of the "blooming, buzzing confusion" of our experience.[21]

Jules: I'm as impressed as Russell by the quality of your oration, Alison, and I bet I'm moved more than he is by your transmutation of constructivism into both a set of questions to pursue and a source of practical insights.

Alison: You are both very kind, but perhaps the Authors would like to begin a new chapter now.

Jules: Who?

---

[21] "The baby, assailed by eyes, ears, nose, skin, and entrails at once, feels it all as one great blooming, buzzing confusion..." William James, *Principles of Psychology*, p. 488.

Interlude

Russell Steadman

In a bend of the Iowa river just below the University was a moist little crayon-green park, gritty and perfect, like a Norman Rockwell postage stamp. It had a child-sized railroad winding through the oaks along the bank, and I could practically live on the train, since my father maintained it as a contribution to the community. A machinist's holiday, he called it, and he loved that little steam engine. Since my parents could never afford much of a getaway in those days, for a long time I thought one's occupation dictated the shape of your holiday: carpenters built sheds, machinists worked on trains, and University housekeeping staff, my mother among them, turned the house upside down, scrubbing the floors and woodwork while their surly sons hauled dusty boxes out of the attic and tracked grit on the rugs. I retreated to the train as often as possible, where with a good book I could enjoy a perfect schoolboy's holiday. To tell the truth, I'm still enjoying it.

Initially, the lure of the academic life for me had nothing at all to do with teaching. That was an annoyance, the part of the job you put up with because it enables you to spend most of your time reading and writing about matters that other people – including most of your students – think are useless or odd. I wasn't alone in this attitude. Most of my fellow graduate students absorbed, ironically by osmosis from our mentors, a deep disdain for teaching. Mastery of the discipline was what counted, and as a first-generation college graduate I was highly sensitive to these expectations, and how the academy enforces them. I've known more than a handful of assistant professors, beloved of students despite, or perhaps because of, their demanding courses, who won prestigious teaching awards only to be denied tenure.

So for me learning to value teaching, and to think seriously about it, came slowly and haltingly. Were it not for some very special friends, in whose hands the profession rises to a fine art, I would probably still be blathering cluelessly at my students, angrily wondering why they don't get it. Some of these friends are actual survivors of my classroom, Alison Bridges chief among them, and to them I owe an enormous debt of gratitude for persisting in the belief that someone of my age could still learn, and even someday, perhaps, learn to teach.

Chapter Three

Between Neutrality and Justice[22]

Is critical thinking a neutral set of skills and dispositions essentially unrelated to any social or moral conclusions? Or is this notion of abstract neutrality itself an ethical problem? If so, honest teaching even of basic cognitive skills should confront the hegemony of unjust relationships, institutions, and conceptual schemes. Are these two notions of criticality – the one neutral, the other always embedded within a social-political framework — strict alternatives, or might there be common ground between them?

Liberating Reason

Alison: We've been speaking quite a lot about the fostering of autonomy – progressively coming to think in a grounded way for oneself -- as a central goal of teaching. I wonder how this relates to the Freirean idea of *liberation*, understood as the sole legitimate aim of pedagogy?[23]

---

[22] An earlier version of this chapter is to be published in *Poverty, Markets, and Justice*, Philosophy Documentation Center, 2011.
[23] Paulo Freire (1921-1997), a Brazilian educator and theorist who ranks among the most influential educational thinkers of the twentieth century. His *Pedagogy of the Oppressed* (1970) and many other works emphasize the social dynamics of learning, and place respectful dialogue among equals as the paramount educational method.

Jules: Be careful not to get me started on Paulo Freire and his followers, Alison! I'm a huge fan of his groundbreaking work on the profoundly political nature of all teaching and learning. Not only would he have liked our emphasis on developing student autonomy, he probably would have encouraged us to push it even further.

Russell: Forgive me, but I get suspicious of anything that comes with a radical *caché*, especially when it promises to push a sensible idea "even further." In my experience, this usually presages an exaggeration to absurdity, especially whenever politics pokes its nose where it doesn't belong.

Alison: Let's try our best to keep it civil, okay? I know you are both good-hearted, but your passion compels me to remind us all that we're here to try to *answer these questions*, not to score points or align ourselves one way or the other with intellectual trends.

Jules: I don't think either Russell or I were on the verge of incivility. But point taken. Let's see what the Freirean, overtly political approach does or does not have to offer us as teachers.

Russell: I'm thinking not much, frankly, but I'm willing to give it its day in court. If you'll try to curb your enthusiasm, Jules, I will endeavor to suppress my skepticism.

Alison: That's the spirit, or as close as we get in a typical classroom at least!

Russell: So that I don't come off as merely reactive, I'll begin with the positive claim that core learning is politically neutral.

And what we call *critical thinking*, or thinking objectively[24] about the products and processes of our own thinking and doing, bespeaks no particular content or political-ideological point of view whatsoever. To be a critical thinker is simply to pursue a life devoted to reason. To ignore this fact courts demagoguery in teaching.

Alison: I take it you are being deliberately provocative.

Russell: I'm just expressing an honest belief. I'm aware some people think otherwise, but by being definite and clear I hope to provoke no more than edifying conversation.

Jules: Actually, Russell, your very words are a tidy example of the ubiquity of political influence in all discourse. Your status as a professor of philosophy, your mastery of analytical thought, and so forth, speak volumes before you open your mouth. You amplify this whenever you express yourself with such rhetorical certainty and authority…

Russell: Oh, don't be silly, Jules. You're choosing to characterize my words that way just because you disagree with me!

Alison: Perhaps a less personalized example would be better.

Jules: Okay. Consider a typical classroom, at any level you like, from kindergarten through graduate school: we can witness variations in the authority a teacher exercises, but the *fact* of authority seems constant.

---

24 Philosophers employ the terms 'objective' and 'subjective' in a specific way. A claim is objective if we possess a public method for investigating whether or not it is true. A claim is subjective if the primary evidence for determining its truth is a matter of individual experience, opinion, or taste. In this usage, "The Earth is round" and "Murder is wrong" are objective claims, whereas "I have a headache" is a subjective claim. Either sort of claim, of course, might be true or false.

Russell: I agree with you, whether it only *seems* to be or *is in fact* constant. The truth is, I suspect the latter, since some kind of authority always informs teacher-student relationships.

Jules: What kind exactly?

Russell: Well, it's never self-serving or arbitrary, and flows from the teacher's greater knowledge of the subject, wider understanding of the analytical tools of the discipline, and sustained experience reasoning well and clearly about the topic at hand.

Jules: You may be right in principle, but in actual practice the teacher's authority *always* has many other features, arising from social status, cultural history, personality, and especially institutional role.

Russell: I take these things to be genuine, if regrettable, intrusions on ideal pedagogical relations, but the best teachers labor to avoid them.

Jules: The Freirean insight is that these influences, which you call regrettable intrusions, are endemic to any real-world teaching situation. Since these power relations and other sources of authority are part of who we are and can never be entirely avoided, we must acknowledge and work with them.

Alison: How would we do that?

Jules: By becoming progressively conscious of the dynamic of authority in the teacher-learner relationship, and use it deliberately in an effort to liberate and empower our students. I suppose this is something like your notion of grounded paternalism.

Russell: Subtract off the revolutionary-sounding phrases, and maybe we're after the same thing.

Jules: I would hope so, but to maintain the fiction that we are approximating your ideal pedagogical relations only serves to *conceal* such "regrettable intrusions," and this invisibility makes them all the more powerful.

Alison: When you say that authoritarian intrusions are endemic and cannot be erased, I take it you do *not* mean to imply that we are helpless in the face of their deterministic force?

Jules: No, of course not. As we become aware of their influence on our thinking, we can make progressively more liberating choices in relation to our students. Why do you ask?

Alison: Because I wonder how it is any different from the Enlightenment emphasis on the power of reason. In fact, your suggestion that we think clearly about what influences our beliefs sounds to me a lot like Russell's description of critical thinking.

Russell: I had the same thought. You seem to want it both ways, Jules. On the one hand, you claim the illegitimate bases of a teacher's authority are ineradicable, so we have no choice but to try to use them for what we see as the good. On the other hand, you seem to presume that the methods of critical thinking can help students eventually liberate themselves from that authority.

Jules: Freirean liberation involves actually bringing about change in human relations and institutional and economic structures, so that students and others are no longer oppressed.

Russell: Well, good luck with that! But do you suppose for a minute that people will ever be free from oppression who cannot think for themselves?

Jules: I suppose not. Critical thinking as you describe it does seem necessary for liberation, but I agree with Freire that it is not by itself sufficient.[25]

Russell: I won't dispute that, and I'm willing to admit that the critical task of overcoming prejudice is one we never wholly complete.

Alison: So it looks like we are in essential agreement after all?

Jules: What about Russell's suggestion that Enlightenment-style critical thinking "bespeaks no particular content or point of view whatsoever"? I would join Freire in rejecting that claim.

Alison: Why do you say that?

Jules: Because everything we say or do bears the mark of our unique, individual perspectives and histories. Maybe we can change or widen our points of view, and with careful attention choose more appropriate or liberating ones, but each of us thinks, speaks, and acts from a perspective that is in some way limited to who we are and where we've been.

Russell: This is old news, Jules. All living organisms, in contrast to gods or disembodied spirits, experience the world from some place or other. But since, as you say, we can with a little effort widen and improve our views, nothing about our original position prevents us from moving toward perfectly general truths about the world.[26]

Jules: No matter how much it improves, your view will always be your view, Russell.

---

25 For a detailed treatment of these issues, see Nicholas C. Burbules and Rupert Berk, "Critical Thinking and Critical Pedagogy: Relations, Differences, and Limits."
26 For an extended defense of this claim, see Thomas Nagel, *The View From Nowhere*.

Russell: I'm entirely willing to take responsibility for my views, especially the improved ones! Look, constructivist tautologies aside,[27] the fact that we must experience the world from some perspective or other tells us absolutely nothing about what we can or cannot know or experience.

Jules: I have already given you and Alison due credit for moving me beyond the most extreme elements of radical constructivism.[28]

Russell: Well, then can we safely infer that you no longer subscribe to the radical relativism or "ontological agnosticism" with which it flirts?

Jules: You may.

Russell: Good. I take it that you are thus no longer shy about saying that we can know something about ourselves and the world?

Jules: Some connotations of the word 'know' still make me uneasy, but I think we can certainly come to *understand* some things about the world and ourselves, yes.

Alison: That's a refreshing distinction, Jules. In my teaching, I am usually less concerned with what my students *know*, purely in terms of data or factual information, than with how they *understand* it, which includes making sense of it, grasping its importance in context, and keeping an open mind. The gerund 'understanding' has a suitable ring of ongoing process and intellectual activity – and by suggesting a particularity of context, it includes the political issues that concern Jules.

---

27 Constructivists of a "radical" stripe often pretend to derive antirealist or relativistic conclusions about knowledge ("I cannot know the way the world really is") from simple tautological premises ("I can only know what I know"). For an analysis of this common fallacy, see David Stove, *The Plato Cult*.
28 See Johnson and Silliman, *Bridges to the World*, especially chapter 15, "Ontological Agnosticism and Solipsism."

Russell: 'Understanding' is a perfectly serviceable term for what contemporary philosophers are after, and I think it's especially appropriate in an educational context where we have defined learning as the intentional acquisition of an ability. There's nothing "post-modern" or especially new about it. In fact, early modern philosophers of knowledge favored the term.[29] Think of Locke's *Essay Concerning Human Understanding*.

Jules: Or Hume's *Enquiry Concerning Human Understanding*. I'm glad we're in agreement, Russell, and with that small terminological caveat, I think we are safe from the threat of any sort of radical relativism.

Alison: What point were you making, then?

Jules: I'm merely defending a *moderately* relativist view: given our unique perspectives on the world, we are always subject to presuppositions, ideas, and influences that we have not yet deconstructed – or if you prefer, thought critically about – so we are never entitled to think we're above politics, especially in relationships as complex as teaching.

Russell: As a healthy statement of fallibility I won't quibble with those claims, Jules. I worry, though, that they might conceal a dangerously slippery slope. Good-hearted, humanist teachers like yourself will surely interpret even "moderate" relativism as *carte blanche* to impart to your students what you take, perhaps even rightly, to be good politics and a sense of social justice.

Jules: Thank you. I struggle to do exactly that.

---

29 See Harvey Siegel, "Gimme That Old-Time Enlightenment Meta-Narrative: Radical Pedagogies (And Politics) Require Old-Fashioned Epistemology (And Moral Theory)."

The Politics of Teaching

Russell: But suppose some teacher's politics were something you or I would find abhorrent – advocating genocide or torture, for example. Would he or she be justified by your principle to teach from that warped perspective?

Alison: I take it your point is that the principle "all teaching is irreducibly political," and the alleged license it gives us to make teaching an overtly political act, seems to embody no necessary boundaries on what sort of politics would be beyond the pale?

Russell: Just so.

Jules: But the principle, as articulated by Freire and others, *does* contain such boundaries, and they are more than enough to constrain any unjust politicization of the classroom or slide into an "anything goes" relativism. The boundaries are built into the very purpose and point of education itself, which is the liberation of students from all arbitrary authority – whether that of the teacher, the culture, or their own insecurities.

Alison: That's a tidy move. If we assume that the principal reason we educate is to free students from any authority but their own informed and autonomous deliberations – another way of framing the development of autonomy we have discussed – perhaps we *could* identify meaningful constraints on what counts as good pedagogical politics, and thus admit overt politics to the classroom in a controlled manner.

Russell: Many, perhaps most teachers and students, do not operate on this assumption, so it will need a rigorous defense before we're done. But even if it were a broadly shared understanding of the end of education, I fear this would not effectively banish our *genocidaire*. Consider a typical middle-class German child in the

1930s, empowered by the friendship and support of Hitler Youth activities, receiving a rigorous and expansive education in music, art, history, languages, mathematics, and so forth, in some of the best public schools in the world.

Jules: But those schools imposed rigid social formalities and curricula, and were strictly elitist and authoritarian to a degree that would shock many of us today.

Russell: True enough, or so I've heard. My point is that nonetheless these schools *did* empower many students in Germany, in effect liberating them from prohibitions on torture and genocide.

Jules: That's clearly not what Freire means by liberation or empowerment!

Alison: Of course it isn't. But Russell has a point. We might even say that the events of September 11, 2001, "liberated" many U.S. politicians and their supporters from previous, long-standing prohibitions on torture and preemptive war.

Jules: Sadly enough.

Alison: Obviously, we need to do more than offer nice-sounding words like 'liberation' and 'student autonomy.' These ideas need specification and defense. And, as Russell would probably agree, their adequate defense can come only from critical thought that seeks objective reasons to prefer one interpretation of liberation or autonomy over another.

Russell: Exactly, Alison. Teaching toward students' autonomy sounds nice, but at the very least we must ensure that the empowerment we foster in them is coherent with the like empowerment of everyone else.

Jules: Freire was influenced by Marx, and by the Liberation Theology movement, so of course he agrees that liberty is socially grounded and justified, rather than simply an individual acquisition. He and his followers are fiercely opposed to the popular model of education as job training for individual advancement or economic development, for example.[30]

Alison: To hear some of our political leaders talk, economic advancement is the only reason they can imagine for supporting schools, and sadly many educators, parents, and students fall into this same trap.[31]

Russell: I hope all teachers agree that learning is its own reward, but we shouldn't go overboard. Liberation from material want, which in our world means being qualified to work and able to find some, is no trivial matter. My father was a machinist and my mother a janitor, and they got their educations where they could find them.

Alison: But Russell, surely you could not have become an intellectual if they had not valued education beyond earning a weekly paycheck?

Russell: They were not unsupportive, and Iowa City was a wonderful place to learn in those days, but I don't think they ever really understood why I didn't do something more obviously practical.

Jules: I think Freire would say this attitude is a measure of their oppression. There's nothing wrong with knowing how to earn a living, of course. But learning and life don't stop with bare

---

30 Jeremy Rifkin explicitly links the worker-training model of education with a reductively individualist notion of autonomy in *The Empathic Civilization*.
31 See Martha Nussbaum, *Not For Profit; Why Democracy Needs the Humanities*.

survival. Alfred North Whitehead affirms that all learning should be useful – for culture and life as well as a living.[32]

Russell: I didn't mean to suggest my parents were narrow people – my mother loved music and books as much as I do, and my father had an inventor's spirit, if limited opportunity to exercise it. I simply hope we can avoid any artificial distinction between some notion of pure education and learning how to make one's way in the world.

Jules: I take it that was Whitehead's point.

Alison: I can agree wholeheartedly, and I wouldn't expect someone influenced by Marx to doubt it.

Jules: Fair enough, so long as we also agree that employment and economic growth are not the *main* point of learning. But let's not lose sight of our target here, namely, Russell's allegation that critical thinking is ideologically neutral, contrasted with the Freirean insight that such an attitude covertly reinforces prevailing structures.

Critical Thinking and Neutrality

Russell: Jules, you and I are hardly ideological soulmates, but the very possibility of our carrying on this conversation presupposes our shared commitment to reason.[33] We often disagree, but it's not just dueling ideologies; we listen to each other, and are persuaded (or not) by the quality of the reasons we give and how clearly we present them. We are to this extent *educated* persons – liberated, autonomous, reasonable, call it what you like.

---

32 "Pedants sneer at an education which is useful ... [But] of course education should be useful, whatever your aim in life. It was useful to Saint Augustine, and it was useful to Napoleon. It is useful, because understanding is useful." Alfred North Whitehead, *The Aims of Education*, p. 2.
33 See Harvey Siegel, *Educating Reason*.

Jules: Do you really think the devotion to "reason" is *not* an ideological stance? Don't even get me started on the history and sociology of science...

Russell: I concede that some people have treated a thing they *called* reason as a rigid ideology, but there's something off about that – reason makes a strange object of fanaticism.

Alison: I would say the social cultivation of reasonableness is a very good thing to be passionate about.

Russell: Sure, passion is important, but I don't think it's reasonable to be blindly fanatical about *anything*, especially reason itself. Critical thinking, properly understood, really does transcend ideology.

Jules: Could you explain why you think so?

Russell: Here's a clear example. One objective feature of reason is its built-in, structural requirement of self-correction. By contrast, no ideological standpoint has this feature, except to the extent that it subjects itself, extra-ideologically, to critical examination.

Jules: This is just the sort of thinking the Freireans resist: setting up Reason-with-a-capital-R as a kind of über-ideology that everyone must worship! Talk about meta-narratives!

Russell: Your overheated rhetoric misses the point. Reason is neither an ideology nor a meta-narrative, whatever that is.[34] It's just a fairly pedestrian set of tools – hammer, saw, measuring tape, chalk line – without which no one could build much of anything substantial.

---

34 Not all meta-narratives are avoidable or inherently oppressive. See Siegel, *Rationality Redeemed? Further Dialogues on an Educational Ideal.*

Jules: If that really were all reason amounted to, how is it that the European colonialists managed to carve up the planet in its name? Reason is no mere hammer; it's a demand for obedience![35]

Russell: I have already conceded that it is possible to misuse a hammer as though it were a weapon, but to do so is anything but reasonable. Someone who views the world as *nothing but* a field of ideological power-plays can't help but interpret the demands of reason in that way, but this reductive view of the world is a mistake

Jules: How so?

Russell: In the first place, the principles of sound reasoning do not originate as a system of ideas in the usual sense: unlike many of our concepts, we do not invent them, we discover them.

Jules: I don't recall ever seeing a piece of reason lying about in nature awaiting discovery! The principles of reason are *our* principles; we actively generate them in the course of thinking about and experiencing the world.

Russell: I smell a red herring, Jules! No doubt the principles of sound reasoning are ours. But they are discoverable features of the world of organized human thought, just as the number *Pi* expresses our discovery of the fixed relationship between the circumference and the diameter of circular things.

Alison: And in the second place?

Russell: This point will seem like a direct affront to Freire's so-called critical pedagogy, I'm afraid. In the same way that correcting

---

[35] For a famous articulation of this view, see Umberto Maturana, "Reality: The Search for Objectivity or the Quest for a Compelling Argument," who reduces all truth claims to demands for obedience (which, of course, has the paradoxical implication of so characterizing his very account of truth).

an error presupposes the existence of a truth, the neutrality of critical thinking is in fact a condition of the possibility of liberatory pedagogy.

Jules: Well, you're right about it being an affront!

Russell: Bear with me. If the social world really were, as some followers of Freire suggest, an arena of *nothing but* competing power blocs and ideologies, its full Hobbesian implications would follow: a war of all against all, life brutal and short, and so on. At that point, only a sovereign power of some sort could bully us into détente.

Alison: A shockingly autocratic and paternalistic result...

Russell: Certainly not a world view that could effectively foster liberation, in its pedagogy or anywhere else.

Jules: I'm not sure Freire actually holds such a simplistic view, but I see that anyone who did would have a problem, according to your reasoning.

Alison: To be fair to the spirit of our conversation, Jules, that last qualifier is out of line. If you understand the reasoning and agree that its conclusion follows, then it's not just Russell's reasoning, but yours as well. I take it that this is part of what he means by the independence of reason.

Jules: Now who's sounding combative?

Alison: I'm not taking sides here. This isn't even *about* sides! But I want to get back to Russell's claim about teaching critical thinking.

Jules: I would expect it to be perfectly clear. If Russell is right to insist that reason is ideologically neutral, it would follow that we can and should teach it that way. He suggested that anything else would be demagoguery.

Alison: I don't think anything of the sort follows.

Russell: You don't?

Alison: Not at all. For one thing, the nature of a topic always underdetermines the teaching methods we need to convey it effectively. History is long, but it would be silly to schedule a longer class period for it on that account. Biology – your field, Jules – has all sorts of creepy, slimy, and infectious features that we don't necessarily replicate in the lesson plan.

Russell: I take your point.

Alison: Good. Secondly, as you both well know from experience, understanding something and being able to teach it are radically independent, in part because it can be difficult to recall empathetically what it was like *not* to understand it. This is why teaching is an art, and, as Russell pointed out earlier, being an expert in your field is not equivalent to being a good teacher of it.

Jules: You can say that again! I've heard this referred to as the "Curse of Knowledge."[36]

Alison: That phrase makes it sound universal or inevitable. I don't think it's so much a curse as a bad habit, arising from an underdeveloped sense of empathy and imagination – the ability to step outside of yourself, listen to others, and craft a narrative trail from their understandings to yours.

---

[36] Chip Heath and Dan Heath in *Made to Stick; Why Some Ideas Die and Others Survive.*

Russell: Those skills do seem to be in short supply in our culture. Most people can't seem to give a stranger adequate directions in their own neighborhoods, as I found out on the way here. But this related insight aside, what conclusion were you about to draw from your two premises?

Alison: Spoken like a true logician.

Russell: I am that, and other things, too.

Alison: I just meant that I admire your skill in articulating the nature of critical thinking while employing it in this very conversation.

Russell: Thank you. But what *was* your conclusion?

Two Notions of Criticality

Alison: My own experience is that trying to teach critical thinking skills without embedding them in some robust content that is familiar and engaging to the students is a disaster. Moreover, we need to draw much of this content from the political and personal stuff of real life, as this is just the area where students will most need to learn how to think clearly and systematically.

Russell: Well, I'm not sure about your last point. These kinds of real-life commitments, along with fraught matters of justice and equity, are precisely where thinking critically is most difficult to do, because we have deep emotional investments in them. You need to learn to garden before you buy the farm…

Alison: Nice metaphor, Russell. But don't you agree that these are the central personal and social issues about which we most need to learn to reason well?

Russell: Yes, of course. We can't omit this content, but I think it is important first to learn the skills on easier issues, and then apply them to emotionally intense matters when the students are more mature.

Alison: And I suspect just when and how to do so is a tactical question about which good teachers can disagree.

Jules: Excuse me, but are you both saying what it sounds to me like you're saying, that you agree with Freire about the profoundly political nature of teaching and learning?

Russell: Not the way I took him to mean it, but maybe in the more limited sense that Alison describes.

Alison: I think I mean to say just that, Jules.

Jules: So it turns out that the alleged neutrality of critical thinking is completely consistent with a pedagogy devoted to liberation and social justice?

Russell: The neutrality of critical thinking is a fact, not an allegation, but if Alison's teacherly instincts are correct, it looks like we can balance these ideas in practice. I must insist, however, that the barest hint of ideological *indoctrination* is an abuse of our authority.

Alison: …and an assault on students' autonomy. We can neither tell students what to think nor bully them into agreeing with us. But this hardly prevents us from expressing and exemplifying our social consciences in the classroom, or explaining the reasoning that we believe leads us to the sense of justice that motivates us.

Jules: In my experience, a heavy-handed approach to such matters backfires anyway. Many students fiercely resist when they think

I'm preaching to them, and reject whatever I say for that reason alone.

Russell: Good for them! Their anti-authoritarian impulse may only be a precursor to thinking critically, but it's a healthy first step.

Alison: I have an intuition about how it happened that you two seemed initially to disagree about critical thinking. You, Russell, use the term 'critical' in something like Kant's sense, don't you?[37]

Russell: Yes. A critique is a systematic investigation and assessment of the strengths, weaknesses, presuppositions, and implications of our concepts.

Alison: More simply put, that sounds like thinking carefully about something.

Russell: Basically, yes. Kant could be wordy.

Alison: Whereas, like Freire, you mean something a little different by critique, don't you Jules?

Jules: I think of critique as a rigorous political-ideological investigation of our knowledge, pedagogy, and many other things, in the context of a systematic criticism of the *status quo*.

Alison: And by 'criticism' you mean thinking carefully about the *status quo* – with the main goal of figuring out what's *wrong* with it?

Jules: There is not, nor is there soon likely to be, a shortage of things wrong with the prevailing power structure that need figuring out and changing.

---

37 See Immanuel Kant, *Critique of Pure Reason*.

Alison: I take it that this negative insight, and accompanying notion of criticism, is just what motivates theorists like Freire. Notice how similar it is in practical content, however, to Russell's more neutral notion of critique, and how as a consequence you might only appear to be at cross-purposes when your actual views and practices are not that far apart.

Russell: I'm still a very long way from Jules's and Freire's radical *chic*.

Alison: I can tell, Russell. But doesn't your commitment to critical thinking as a process of systematic questioning reveal to you any injustice in our world, or the need to do something about it?

Russell: I'll take that as a rhetorical question.

Alison: And I'll take *that* as a concession to Jules's insistence that the classroom is not, in this important sense, a neutral zone.

Russell: It's impossible to remain neutral when a heavy dose of critical thinking unearths some ugly truths about the *status quo*. Clearly, something's wrong and needs changing. But imagining a better future and a way to get there are further tasks. Critical thinking seems most like a tool for diagnosing error, not projecting possible remedies.

Jules: And recognizing the ugliness of those truths belies your purported neutrality.

Russell: Perhaps, but objective truths they remain, discoverable by a clear-headed analysis of the facts.

Interlude

Alison Bridges

Trees are my earliest memory of the southern Vermont hills. Everyone likes the fall colors, but for me the real grip of the place is in November. Stark tree fingers poke at the sky, already a hard winter cobalt, the only sound a windy arpeggio through twigs and branches. The winter trees now freely orchestrate the wind, having waited all summer and fall to brush off the leaves and improvise.

I learned piano, in large part, despite my parents. Many children resist music lessons, but I found myself badgering them into letting me play. Money was scarce on our small farm, and since pianos are costly beasts, we borrowed a dusty old upright from my Uncle, and made sure it was in tune. They were also concerned about the cost of the lessons, and were convinced that I wouldn't practice enough. So I got a paper route to earn money, and practiced almost every night after supper until they sent me to bed. To this day I'm not sure whether they really didn't want me to play the piano, or just knew I would resist whatever they said and were deliberately goading me into proving them wrong. I was always a willful child. If they really were trying to get me to motivate myself, it was an effective trick, one I will admit to playing from time to time on my own students.

My willfulness, the insistent trees, and my devotion to making music eventually drove me to my next artistic obsession, the study of literature. That trajectory may not follow by formal inference, but it has a vigorous poetic logic. Since my options at that point were either (1) lonely, starving artist or (2) teacher, my subsequent career choice followed naturally, and I took on the teaching profession with the same dogged passion as I had the piano and George Eliot. With time, it has become the center of my life. Much as I love to read, write poetry, and make music, I am endlessly fascinated by the social dynamic of learning and teaching. As an opportunity for improvisation and joy, it's a gold mine, though I find it occasionally contains some duller rocks as well.

Chapter Four

Between Structure and Creativity

We rightly value creativity in learning, but it seems at odds with memorizing, imitating, or studying existing concepts and objects of all sorts, activities which often seem not only uncreative, but antagonistic to creativity. The paradox resolves when we realize that these activities provide the frameworks within which creativity becomes possible. Seen in this light, close study and memorization of existing material can serve as an engaging and fruitful platform for creative improvisation.

Creativity and Imagination

Jules: This one fact is undeniable: imagining alternatives to the *status quo* is no easy task for our students, who have been trained to internalize and repeat prevailing social and political realities, like first-year art students faithfully copying shadows cast by plaster cubes.

Russell: That's an odd analogy, especially coming from one of my more artsy colleagues. Do you really want to conflate the act of parroting someone else's ideas and carefully attending to the details of the world around us?

Jules: Well, of course I don't. In fact, I think the kind of imaginative creativity that accompanies the arts is central to all learning.

Alison: Or to creative imagination itself...

Russell: How do you think imagination and creativity are related?

Alison: Creativity seems to me to be a concrete application of imagination. A creative solution to a mathematical problem, for example, is the publicly accessible *product* of the capacity to imagine a number of possible solutions. Its creativity resides in grounding imaginative possibilities in an elegant or novel suggestion that works.

Jules: But couldn't we equally say that imagination flows from creativity? Isn't a creatively imaginative act equally an imaginatively creative one?

Russell: There's no dispute here. Alison's claim that creativity is a form of imagination is consistent with feedback between the two over time. Technology, to take another example, is both an application of our thinking and something that can in turn greatly impact our thinking.

Alison: That sounds about right to me. Writing is an application of thinking, too, and obviously affected by it, just as time spent laboring over my prose can have a positive effect on my thinking. Despite the reciprocity, it still seems to me that imagination is more basic than creativity.

Russell: But surely not as basic as the biological disposition and capacity for play, from which the imagination grows.

Alison: Very playful, Russell!

Russell: Don't forget, I have kids, and I just finished reading the late Denis Dutton's thought-provoking treatise on the evolution of human taste.[38]

---

[38] Denis Dutton, *The Art Instinct*.

Alison: I like your taste in books.

Russell: Thanks. Again, I suspect there are complex interconnections between play, imagination, and creativity, but at least as far as the latter two are concerned, the categorical relation seems to be this: creativity is properly a subset of imagination, such that everything that is creative is part of imagination, but not everything that is part of imagination is creative. If we think of it in terms of nested circles representing categories, creativity resides wholly within the larger circle of imagination.

Alison: So, even more simply, creativity is to imagination as "good student" is to "students."

Jules: And our job is to expand the smaller circle to become coterminous with the larger one.

Russell: And then all students will be above average, I suppose! When all of our students are advanced students, who will be left to copy the plaster cubes?

Learning by Imitating

Jules: Okay, let me clarify what I meant by my off-hand comment about art students. Imitation is surely a fundamental skill, but its primary function is to serve as the basis for developing the autonomous, creative products of more advanced studies. As Max Wyman writes:

> ...engagement with artistic creativity develops the ability to think creatively in ways that significantly enlarge the educational experience. It encourages the flexible, nuanced thinking that will be an essential requirement of any innovative response to the challenges we face. It makes

us see our world in fresh ways, encourages suppleness of mind. Doubt is cast on our most comfortable perceptions. We learn the art of adaptability.[39]

Russell: I like what Wyman says. And, as I see it, those more advanced skills and habits should be the focus of our efforts to teach college-age students. They can brush up on the basics on their own, in remedial classes, or go back to grammar school!

Alison: Hold on, Russell. The early years are much more than a training ground for later, genuinely autonomous and creative acts. In fact, as we have earlier observed with respect to autonomy, imagination and creativity don't emerge fully formed in adults, but are developmental products of sound, lifelong pedagogical practices.

Jules: I think that helps explain my adult preference for non-representational art. Copying is one basic skill. Moving beyond what is immediately given to the senses is another, deeper thing entirely. As Einstein supposedly said, "Knowledge is limited. Imagination encircles the world."

Alison: Easy for him to say! No doubt he valued the imagination as a source of new and unexpected knowledge. Likewise, to think for oneself is always in a way to go beyond simple imitation. But it seems to me you have prematurely condemned the role of "copying" or imitating in art and education.

Russell: True enough. Show me students who can copy their teachers and I'll show you very strong students indeed!

Jules: Or very capable imitators of potentially faulty methods and content, and not necessarily prepared to think for themselves!

---

39 Max Wyman, *The Defiant Imagination: Why Culture Matters*, p. 7.

Russell: I was obviously imagining decent and right-thinking teachers who model critical thinking as we have defined it. Don't we want students to develop these abilities, too?

Alison: Well, there's a big difference between developing the ability to think critically and *copying* the activities of critical thinkers. As Jules's has convinced me in our earlier conversations, knowing something is never a simple matter of mirroring the world. Even successful mimicry requires careful attention to detail, lots of practice, and a certain degree of interpretation.

Jules: Right. Critical thinkers aren't just clever mimics, after all. They really can and do think critically!

Russell: That's what I meant to say, of course.

Alison: So Jules, what's the educational counterpart to non-representational art?

Jules: Learning that has moved beyond what is immediately given or basic to our minds, just as abstract, nonrepresentational works of art redirect our aesthetic attention away from what is immediately present to the senses.

Russell: For instance?

Alison: Like the kind of language-mastery required to produce literature, in contrast to a mere collection of grammatical sentences?

Jules: That's the sort of thing I had in mind. Notice the artistry and creativity literature demands of us, the perceptivity and nuance, the recombination of mundane elements to reach for something sublime.

Russell: But the sentences from which we form literature had better be grammatical on the whole – or if they're not, the author should know precisely why! Literature doesn't get us *beyond* grammar, anymore than so-called abstract art transcends representation. Rather, they employ and manipulate it to great effect. And neither does this conversation, or those of our more advanced students, allow us to neglect the basic elements of critical thinking.

Jules: Don't get me wrong. I don't want to suggest that copying, or realistic representation in art generally, is a bad thing. As Clive Bell maintains, it's just irrelevant to an object's status as notable art.[40]

Russell: Notable art is non-representational?

Jules: No, I just maintain with formalists like Bell that its capacity to represent is irrelevant. Notable art may or may not represent anything.

Russell: Give me one example of a notable work of art that fails entirely to represent anything and lunch is on me!

Jules: Easy enough, so get your credit card ready. Jackson Pollock's drip paintings, like John Cage's silent work *4:33*, have no apparent representational content. Their artistic properties are strictly a matter of significant or ideal form.

Russell: Remind me never to go to an art museum or concert with you, Jules!

Jules: Do you not accept these as examples of non-representational art? Or are you just expressing conservative tastes?

Russell: Maybe both. Some things ought to be conserved, like the

---

40 Clive Bell, "Art as Significant Form."

notion that all good art is representational. How else could it move an audience? I'll say this: if either Pollock's or Cage's work is art, then it definitely represents something!

Alison: There's no obvious content to Pollock's drip-paintings, Russell. They seem only accidentally to represent anything beyond themselves, wouldn't you say – as clouds may sometimes, but only incidentally, look like sheep?

Russell: If that's true, then Pollock's line-paintings represent, among other things, the power and significance of non-representation.

Jules: What kind of representation is that, Russell? Leave it to a philosopher to suggest that something that fails to represent actually succeeds in representing nothingness! You just don't want to buy lunch! Non representational art isn't any kind of failed representation – it doesn't represent *at all*.

Russell: Look, as all good artists know, nothingness, or absence of direct representation, is an element of all art. Consider empty spaces in visual art and architecture, the artistic value of what's not said in poetry and literature. Cage's musical folly aside, where would music be without its silent moments? One big cacophonous chord!

Alison: This seems right, Russell. My own jazz piano studies are always emphasizing the power of silence, of delayed or implied notes, of saying more with less.

Jules: I rather like where you're going with this, too, Russell. But how can you now call Cage's silent work "musical folly"?

Russell: Simply because absence of representation can never be complete. There must be some vehicle of representation – in this case organized sound. Missing this basic ingredient, Cage's work exceeds the sensible limits of musical composition, just as nonexistent paintings, sculptures, buildings, or dance troupes would do the same for other artistic domains.

Jules: But performed in a concert hall with musicians, instruments, lights, a stage and an audience, Cage's four minutes and thirty-three seconds of silence forced us to reconsider what we think music really is! This was pedagogical genius on a cultural scale!

Russell: I will perhaps surprise you by granting that extravagant claim for the work, if you will admit that in making it you concede my point about representation. *4:33* frames music conceptually by refusing to be music, even though it's in a musical context. It goes one step past the boundary of what can count as music – and in so doing reminds us of the limitations of formal musical settings. In this sense the piece is indeed representational, as are Pollock's enigmatic drippings.

Jules: That interpretation of Cage is just clever enough, I might owe *you* lunch!

Alison: You surprise me, Russell, by having thought so much about the boundaries of music, and you may even be right. But if I may summarize what we've lately agreed: critical, nuanced, autonomous, and creative thinking all build upon and reflect the basic, foundational elements of thought and perception including language, sensory input, and logic.

Educating Taste

Jules: Maybe our disagreements about Cage and Pollack simply reflect distinct aesthetic tastes which, as everyone knows, reside in the eye of the beholder.

Russell: Now you're just trying to weasel your way out of buying lunch. Taste not only evolves, as Dutton suggests, but can and must be educated. Otherwise, it simply devolves to immediate pleasure. Studying complex music, for example, can liberate us from the tyranny of unexamined taste and opinion.[41]

Jules: Who are we to question the legitimacy of others' tastes?

Russell: We're three teachers discussing the merits of untutored, uncritical thoughts of all kinds, including tastes in art, that's who we are!

Alison: Russell's claim that we can or ought to educate some of our tastes does not entail that relatively untutored tastes are illegitimate, Jules.

Russell: You always were one of my best logic students, Alison.

Jules: Logical or not, calling someone's tastes "uneducated" is a pretty straightforward condemnation, in my book. Certainly it's a clear challenge to a person's autonomy!

Russell: Sort of reminds me of your assessment of drawing 101...

Alison: Hold on a second. So long as we don't confuse trivial tastes – say, preferences in flavors of ice cream – with manifest tastes in more complex and important venues like art, we're in no danger of arbitrarily imposing our views on each other.

Russell: Absolutely. Since there's always more to learn about the arts, there's always room for educating our tastes.

Jules: Isn't it our understanding or appreciation of the arts that stands to evolve here, not our tastes?

---

41 Peter Kalkavage, "The Neglected Muse: Why Music is an Essential Liberal Art."

Alison: I suppose that is a useful distinction in this context. I can imagine learning a lot about some domain of human experience without it having much effect on my tastes.

Russell: Sure, while raising my kids, I learned a lot about contemporary children's programming on television, but I still prefer the cartoons and shows from the sixties.

Jules: I would have expected philosophers categorically to oppose the "boob tube."

Russell: I only object to mindlessness in certain contexts, Jules.

Alison: Okay, before this gets any more heated, let me suggest a terminological distinction that might help move our conversation forward.

Jules: Please do.

Alison: The word 'taste' alone doesn't do justice to the experiential gulf that separates some activities from others. Some tastes, we can agree, are trivial preferences for one sensation over another – like tastes in ice cream. In other contexts, like education or the arts, the term 'taste' elliptically designates our current state of understanding or appreciation for much more complex and consequential matters.

Russell: That makes sense, Alison. In many contexts, usually those with the most far-reaching implications for the good life, the word 'taste' is downright misleading or wrong. To say that I prefer the first movement of Mozart's *Piano Concerto no. 21* to the third, for example, is hardly synonymous with "my tastes incline me to the former."

Jules: No? It seems to me it is to say just that. Your tastes allow you to say that you prefer the one movement to the other.

Russell: That is true in one sense, but misleading because cryptic and incomplete. Alison's point, as I see it, is that our preferences for one over the other amount to more than mere spontaneous preferences for one sensation over another.

Alison: Exactly. We needn't deny our untutored attraction to aspects of Mozart's compositions, but there is always an element of learned appreciation, given the complexity of its form, its history, and our own.

Jules: I have read that some critics in his own time thought his music was strangely complex and unpleasant, so you must be right that we're all on an invisible cultural learning curve.

Russell: The same process operates in other areas of human concern, like ethics and education. My preference for critical thinking or the Golden Rule, for example, is not a matter solely of taste, even though untutored sensations of joy and surprise always accompany my experience of those domains.

Alison: That's right; the simple pleasures often co-exist happily with the new, more complex ones. I think we can understand on that basis not only the evolution of your appreciation of artistic creativity, Jules, but the very nature of ethics as a discipline.

Jules: How so?

Alison: Well, as I see it, the complexities of various warring ethical theories all have their source in the same basic intuitions or thoughts, like the wrongness of taking an innocent life.[42]

Russell: Well put! Just as Escher's elaborate artwork not only presupposes, but also reflects, the basic elements of perspective captured by art students drawing their first cubes, so a theoretical

---

42 See Silliman, *Sentience and Sensibility*.

edifice limning the nuances of right and wrong has everyday morality as its raw material. These certainly are matters of taste, but also of perceptivity, reason, and dialogue.

Jules: I withdraw my comment about imposing tastes. It's pretty clear to me now that cultivating a taste in our students for critical thinking is no kind of veiled condemnation of their current abilities, but a necessary nudge in the direction of greater intellectual autonomy and, in turn, creativity.

Alison: Another welcome moment of agreement.

Pedagogical Improvisations

Jules: Alison, do you think your interest in jazz piano has any implications for education?

Alison: Okay, I guess it's time for me to put my own preferences on the line. As I see it, improvisation is a special kind of creativity.

Russell: I must admit that I don't know much about musical improvisation, but isn't jazz essentially spontaneous and free?

Jules: …almost like the free exercise of the musical imagination, absent any particular content or form?

Alison: Well, aside from some rather extreme and I think marginally engaging examples of so-called "free jazz," you're both offering more of a caricature than an accurate description of jazz.

Russell: We all have our weaknesses!

Alison: Perfectly understandable. The common perception of jazz as entirely undisciplined, even chaotic, quickly fades after a bit of experience with or training in the genre. Jazz is a rigorous creative application of imagination. Indeed, it now strikes me as a perfect example of the distinction between immediate sensation and educated opinion we've been talking about.

Russell: So what is jazz, then?

Alison: I think we best understand jazz as relatively spontaneous, yet constrained, musical creativity.

Russell: Spontaneous *and* constrained? That sounds just a little paradoxical to me!

Alison: Suitably, I think, since some kind of powerful tension is at the heart of both creativity and improvisation.[43] In each case we strive to be productively imaginative, to combine internal freedom with external constraint. Jazz improvisation is the creative manipulation of a fluid set of rules, expectations, and conventions.

Jules: I see. This is analogous to what we have said elsewhere – that critical thinking is always critically thinking *about* something, and by reference to the rules of rhetoric and logic.

Russell: Or likewise that student autonomy is always grounded in, or constrained by, principles of rational thought and action.

Jules: And that it is deeply rooted in mature emotion, neither inconsistent with nor reducible to such rational thought.

Alison: Exactly, on all counts!

Jules: So what makes jazz "relatively spontaneous"?

---

[43] See Alfonso Montuori, "The Complexity of Improvisation and the Improvisation of Complexity: Social Science, Art, and Complexity."

Alison: It's like critical thinking. Just as a "habit" of critical thinking[44] flows from its regular use, after a lifetime of practice and study, jazz improvisers can create new and beautiful music in the moment.

Russell: I suppose the same is true of the well trained athlete, who needs to be able to react instantly and creatively to unpredictable turns in the game.

Alison: Absolutely. In fact, unlike actors reciting a script, we seem to be improvising our way through this conversation, offering what are more or less innovative or creative thoughts within the obvious constraints of an ongoing discussion.

Jules: I suppose those boundaries include those of our shared language, cultural norms, and the rules of rational discourse.

Alison: Not to mention civility, respect, and simple courtesy!

Russell: Very creative! I'm beginning to wonder if we ever *stop* improvising. So I guess my only question now is, why do you say that improvisation is a subset of creativity? Maybe they're just synonymous.

Alison: Well, I suppose that is possible. But let me continue to improvise and try out this line of thought on you two. Jules, the passage you just quoted from Max Wyman reminded me of my own current view of improvisation as an innovative, productive response to complexity.

Jules: Yes. He suggests that creativity in particular "encourages flexible, nuanced thinking [in] response to the challenges we face." He writes further of a "suppleness of mind" and an "art of adaptability."

---

[44] See Harvey Siegel, *Rationality Redeemed?*

Alison: That all sounds to me like improvisation. Consider again the relations between imagination and creativity. As a concrete application of the imagination, creativity, occupies a smaller circle within the larger category of the imagination. Some imaginative moments – inchoate dream states, for example – are not particularly creative.

Russell: I guess we need to dig beneath the surface of this metaphor. What makes an act of the imagination creative – that is, what makes it more or less "concrete?"

Alison: I would say that the mental act of entertaining a thought – the imagination – becomes concrete, and hence potentially creative, when we deliberately use it for some other purpose beyond merely having a thought.

Jules: The way dream analysis is the concrete psychoanalytic application of dream states?

Alison: That's a good example of what I have in mind. Or, even closer to our current concerns, we can understand critical thinking as a rational approach to thinking in some concrete context or other.

Russell: I agree. Critical thinking is creative down to its very bones. So, is improvisation a further "concretization" of creativity?

Alison: I'm beginning to regret using the term concrete, to the extent that it suggests excessive heaviness or intransigence. But I think what you say is about right.

Jules: In other words, improvisation as a kind of creativity occupies a smaller circle within the medium-sized circle of creativity?

Alison: Yes. Improvisation is a kind – or application – of creativity, just as creativity is an application of the imagination.

Russell: What kind of creativity is improvisation?

Alison: I think we rightly think of ourselves as improvising, not just in music but in our lives generally, whenever we are able to think or act creatively in the face of uncertain conditions.

Russell: Well, that makes good sense to me. Just the other day I was driving to Logan Airport for the first time in years, and I suddenly found myself faced with a set of construction detours leading me away from the city.

Jules: I don't know anyone who likes driving through Boston, except maybe some hardcore Bostonians. What did you do?

Russell: I improvised!

Jules: Uh huh.

Russell: I was going to be late picking up my sister at the airport. So I just pulled over and called her cell.

Jules: That's an understanding of improvisation? Remind me never to go to a jazz concert with you!

Alison: Okay, stay calm. Look at our three circles. Improvisation falls inside creativity, which is in turn part of imagination. Like most complex states, improvisation comes in degrees. To improvise is to be a creative problem-solver. But the important thing to notice is that each circle is successively less "unconstrained," open, or free.

Russell: So it's the imagination that's spontaneous and free, not jazz.

Alison: Right. The scope of the imaginative is limited only by, well, our imaginations, which in turn arise from the richness and depth of our experiences.

Jules: And creative uses of the imagination – like critical thinking – always place certain constraints on our thinking and involve specific contexts. Obviously, we are not free to think whatever we like when thinking critically.

Alison: And improvisation in turn involves finding creative solutions to particular, yet uncertain, conditions.

Jules: So Russell's call to his sister wasn't creative after all?

Alison: Logic demands that it was, at least of a mundane sort, since improvisation is an application of creativity. That Russell was being at least minimally creative follows from describing improvisation as a kind of creativity. I just see it as a unique kind, one that's best suited to unforeseeable, evolving circumstances. In fact, I have this favorite passage from Mary Catherine Bateson taped to the wall above my piano:

> Men and women confronting change are never fully prepared for the demands of the moment, but they are strengthened to meet uncertainty if they can claim a history of improvisation and a habit of reflection.[45]

Russell: I like that a lot. Whether it's a proper subset of, or synonymous with, creativity, improvisation has certainly been our constant companion in these discussions. I never know precisely what to expect or say next! But I always find myself with an enriched and strengthened understanding as a consequence of our exchanges.

Alison: That is the beauty and thrill of improvising. I love immersing myself in a relatively spontaneous mixture of melodic, rhythmic, and harmonic moves that at once honor and push against the constraints of an instrument or a musical idea. This is one of life's most rewarding challenges.

---

45 Mary Catherine Bateson, *Peripheral Visions: Learning Along the Way*, p6.

Jules: I hear the passion in your words, Alison, just as I always appreciate the beauty of your playing. But we seem to have drifted some distance from our central theme. What precisely can we, as educators, do with these insights?

Russell: I feel sufficiently inspired to take a stab at that question, and my answer sounds like a remix of Alison's insights and yours:

> *teaching is continually improvisatory, as it demands an empathetic, creative response to each emerging moment in the relationship between the teacher, the students, and the material.*

Jules: If you're right, Russell, the power and value of our rewards as teachers grow along with the challenges we embrace. Some of the best things in life, contrary to the overrated cliché, are neither free nor easy.

Alison: That reminds me of something my favorite jazz pianist, the late Michel Petrucciani, once said to an over-effusive interviewer: "I'm no genius, I just practice a lot."

Jules: Well, I've heard Petrucciani's music, and there *is* a kind of elusive, almost mysterious quality to his music. I think he was just being modest.

Alison: I'm inclined to agree, Jules. Perhaps his genius is a product of the right kind of "practice" – an integration of repetition, interpretation, and creativity.

Jules: And there's a lesson there for our students, who often seem to reduce practice to its first moment, repetition.

Russell: I must say that I've learned something new here – and, as usual, that hasn't been easy. Most of what we do – both as students and teachers – involves addressing one kind of problem or another, many of which often surprise us by their stubborn resistance or complexity. I am now convinced that improvisation, understood as a creative, often deeply satisfying response to those challenging, unexpected moments in our lives, is central to all teaching and learning.

Alison: Yes, and I'm beginning to see how the improvisatory aspect of learning fits with the need to learn both content and structure. A teacher's task, as Whitehead reminds us, is to adjust the principles of freedom and discipline so that they correspond to natural changes in a student's developing personality.[46]

---

[46] Alfred North Whitehead, *The Aims of Education*, pp. 30-1.

Interlude

Jules Randolph Govier

Many are called, as they say, but few are chosen, and there have been more than a few bumps in the pursuit of my passion for teaching. I had heard there was a need for science teachers; I always enjoyed biology, and was certain it could be taught in a more agreeable fashion, so I sought secondary certification in that field. For me, the joy of teaching is all about inspiring and empowering students, relating to them individually, and responding to them as persons in relation to the subject matter. A rigid, test-focused curriculum puts severe constraints on the flexibility one can exercise, and I found myself as disaffected as my students almost daily. I thought perhaps at the post-secondary level, where students are at least technically adults, I would have more freedom to teach with imagination. After still more post-graduate work and the generous, if unexpected, guidance of my friend Russell Steadman, I now find myself up against a whole new set of intellectual and pedagogical challenges.

The truth is, classroom teaching has never come close to living up to what I imagined it could be. I accept some of this as inevitable, just as I eventually learned that no one ever has a real, live conversation as intense, brilliant, and delightful as those Plato portrays in his dialogues. We all must learn to accept the limitations of reality languishing as it does in the shadow of great fiction and idealized imagination. But my conversations with Alison and Russell are often pretty remarkable, while I find myself drained and depressed after most days of teaching. It begins to occur to me that I might look for a way to be a teacher outside such formal settings. Perhaps I could teach guitar, or sailing, or some other craft where students come ready-made with the desire to train and learn. It's not clear how I will make a living this way, but I'm not sure how many more years I can spend supplying my students with both the course content and most of their enthusiasm for learning it.

Chapter Five

Between Showing and Telling

Is there a consistent interpretation of Plato's character Socrates that might provide a powerful model for all teaching? Is there a Socratic method that could help to resolve pedagogical dilemmas about leading or guiding students while respecting their autonomy as learners? What does this model tell us about the role of deception in teaching?

A New Socratism?

Alison: Wait, whose idea was this heading? When did Socrates come up?

Jules: I have no idea where it came from, but I discussed Plato and Socrates in some detail in my dissertation, so I might be able to help figure out the Authors' intentions.

Russell: Let's not get distracted by a theological discussion of whether there are or are not Authors who created us and influence our every word and thought. Whoever put that heading there, I can only guess it's supposed to encapsulate what we've been saying about autonomy and critical thinking.

Alison: Perhaps the Authors also have in mind popular references to Socrates as a model for critical thinking. But I don't get the significance of the question mark.

Jules: I think I do. Socratism as an emblem of enlightened learning would be a fine Authorly intention, if the matter of interpreting the historical Socrates, and Plato's use of him as a literary character, weren't so vastly complicated. It can be dangerous simply to borrow someone's name for your own agenda – look at the arrogant bullying they call the "Socratic Method" in some law schools. It's an embarrassment!

Russell: I know something of the philosophical literature on these matters, and you're right, Jules, it's got lots of problems and is far too easy to oversimplify. I would be willing to bet that most teachers simply equate the "Socratic Method" with asking a lot of questions. But as Alison likes to remind us, our immediate purposes are more practical. Maybe we don't need to resolve all the interpretive nuances.

Alison: Not all, surely, but I don't see how we can settle *a priori* how much detail we need, without discussing at least some of it. Besides, though I'm nobody's idea of a scholar of ancient philosophy, I am a devoted reader of Plato's dialogues. No mere philosopher, Plato is a major literary figure as well.

Russell: Out of respect for our friendship I will take that "mere philosopher" crack as the joke I'm sure you intend, Alison.

Alison: Keep your humor dry, Russell!

Russell: Since you feel strongly about this, Jules, how would you like to encapsulate what you take to be the relevant issues for us in a mini-lecture?

Jules: That's not my usual style, really.

Alison: True, but it's a good suggestion, Jules. Just imagine you're composing another of your wonderful long letters.

Jules: Well, I'll give it a try. I'll need a little while to gather my thoughts.

Alison: Take as long as you like. Russell, could you get us another round of coffee?

Russell: French roast for you, I recall. Cream or sugar?

Alison: Just a drop of soymilk, and I'll take a croissant, if one of you will eat half.

Russell: Jules?

Jules: I'm all set with my tea, thanks... Okay, I have a few notes, so here goes.

> I take the question before us to be the suitability of Socrates and his conversational methods as models for teaching and learning. By 'Socrates' here we must mean not so much the historical person, about whom we have only fragmentary and conflicting accounts,[47] but rather the Socrates we encounter as a character in Plato's dialogues. It seems fair to say that, while this character clearly does not always speak for Plato, he

---

[47] The comic playwright Aristophanes parodies Socrates in *The Clouds* in 423 b.c.e. as an outrageous, sophistic fraud and dangerous corrupter of youth, a characterization that may well have contributed to his execution in 399. More than a half century later, the Athenian general Xenophon composes dialogues in which Socrates appears as a kindly old gentleman full of wise sayings who is patient with the young. Neither Aristophanes nor Xenophon perceives much of what Plato saw – or partly invented – as a complex but coherent Socratic philosophical and pedagogical method.

certainly explores questions of interest to Plato about teaching, learning, and other matters, and seems to represent Plato's idealization of a process of dialogical exploration.[48] This image is the root of Socrates' durability in our historical imagination.

Let me enumerate, then, five characteristics of Socratic pedagogy that we might want to emulate:

- First, he is tireless, always and everywhere prepared for a serious conversation, and willing to talk, patiently, with anyone at all. This is more meritocratic than purely egalitarian, since he sets the bar quite high – it is no casual pastime to participate in a conversation with Socrates. The only qualification for having a Socratic conversation is an earnest desire to do so, but it's a demanding choice.

- Second, Socrates never claims to possess or dispense knowledge, but only to seek it – explicitly disavowing with his protestations of *aporia*[49] any settled, definitive understanding of important subjects. Thus in his conversations with young men he is solicitous of their opinions, seeks their comprehension and concurrence on each move in the argument, and chooses topics

---

48 The apocryphal *Second Letter* says "… I myself have never written anything on these subjects, and there is and will be no book by Plato, but those which now bear his name belong to a Socrates become fair and young" (314C). This in part echoes a passage in the more likely authentic *Seventh Letter* (341C). Since the character Socrates is famous in Plato's dialogues for his physical ugliness and typically advanced age, the author presumably means that the works embody an idealized Socratic personality, intellectual attractiveness, and method. The writings "belong" to this idealized Socrates in two senses: that they dialogically explore philosophical matters rather than propounding doctrines, and that Plato himself never speaks in them.

49 *Aporia*, or Socratic ignorance, is neither a simple lack of knowledge nor a deflective skepticism, but rather acknowledges our lack of full understanding as something for which we seek a cure. It yokes the principles of intellectual humility and intellectual honesty to a relentless and rigorous drive to learn Socrates takes its acknowledgement as a necessary first step to genuine inquiry.

and examples closely tailored to their interests and concerns. In this aporetic, intellectually humble stance he disparages the image of a teacher as arrogant know-it-all, lording it over his students. We should be cautious not to confuse *aporia*, however, with not being a keen observer of the world, human nature, and the personalities of his conversants. Or even with having strong views about things – quite the reverse. In these respects Socrates knows a lot, and freely deploys his knowledge in conducting his pedagogical conversations.

- Third, and as a consequence of this second point, Socrates actively encourages his companions not only to think for themselves, but to do so with rigorous, self-reflective honesty, and at indefinite length. These encouragements reflect the attitudes and dispositions we call critical thinking. The idea that curiosity is a natural good to cultivate, and that we can never presume to have finished inquiring once and for all, is an inspiration to those of us who view education as concerned with far more important things than simply job skills and employability, and certainly not confined to childhood. The culture at large desperately needs such inspiration.

- Fourth, the character Socrates remains a personable, humorous, complex human being despite his utter devotion to teaching and learning for their own sakes. He can even be manipulative, ironic, and infuriatingly disingenuous when it suits his pedagogical purposes, though it is a *principled* disingenuity, if there can be such a thing, aimed at benefiting his students. Plato presents his character as a complete person, who never seems like an automaton or narrow-minded scholar lacking wider human concerns. We might take this as a rebuke to hyperspecialization and unnecessary technicality in learning. If the aim is to help students become, not competent ciphers, but expansively whole persons, it makes sense that the teacher would model such wholeness.

- Fifth, Socrates' pedagogical model would thus emphasize characterological development over technical training, though of course the two are far from exclusive. The point is that, whatever overt content one is learning, a nurturing interpersonal relationship between teacher and students is paramount. In his *Seventh Letter*, Plato speaks of the special camaraderie of the learning relationship. He seems to regard this pedagogical companionship, or *sunousia*,[50] as equal in importance to reason itself in the experience of learning.

Alison: Bravo, Jules! Nice bullet points.

Russell: Well done indeed, my boy.

Jules: I lifted some of that straight from my thesis. I'm sorry that the compression of the lecture form makes the language a bit dense. I would never speak that way except among friends and colleagues.

Alison: I'm glad you did, though, since we are among friends. I know you take very seriously Socrates' insistence on discussion rather than debate, and on the importance of a special kind of companionship in learning, but your summary is a good basis for further discussion.

---

50 Literally "being together." Larger even than the dialogical method, the interpersonal experience of *sunousia* in an educational context seems to be at the heart of Plato's contention that discursive learning, reasoning as a process, is not the only, or even the highest aim of learning. Rather, reasoning carefully, in company with others, prepares the ground for comprehension or insight (*noesis*) of the most important things (Good, Beauty, Justice…), which he suggests may not be susceptible to direct discourse (see *Seventh Letter*, 344B).

Jules: I am convinced that learning is more than simply a discursive or cognitive process. It is also deeply and irreducibly affective and interpersonal. Lectures seem so *im*personal to me.

Russell: But surely this conversation we're having now, *including* your mini-lecture, has that interpersonal quality. I mean to say, I really think there is value in *several* modes of presentation, and even in the variation itself.

Jules: I'll always vote for pluralism, but I'm afraid I've only given half the speech that's called for, and I'm pretty sure I'm not up to composing the rest of it.

Socratic Problems

Alison: I wondered about that. You initially expressed doubts about Socrates as a label or model for pedagogy, but your talk only emphasized the merits. We still have to unpack that pesky question mark.

Russell: Just to show you both that I'm a pluralist, too, we'll do it together. Could you clarify and defend your last point, about *sunousia*? I can't see how Plato really thinks something like *Gemürtlichkeit*[51] is equal in importance to reasoning itself!

Alison: I'd say he does, if we take seriously what Socrates says at the end of Book Six of the *Republic*, about how we only know things like Justice, Beauty, and the Good through a kind of direct intellectual intuition. Reason can't get us there directly, and it prepares us mainly by teaching us to admire and emulate someone whose perception and judgment are more developed than our own.

---

51 Famously difficult to translate, *Gemürtlichkeit* describes a certain kind of fellow-feeling or camaraderie thought to be characteristic of Bavarian folk culture. By invoking the connotation of jovial men in hunting lodges wearing Lederhosen, drinking great draughts of beer, and slapping each other on the shoulders, Russell at once lampoons the importance of *sunousia* and seeks to domesticate it.

Russell: This just sounds like mysticism to me, and antithetical to reason. If Plato thought that, he must momentarily have become confused about his own commitment to rationality.

Jules: I agree with Alison. I don't think Plato's Socrates is being mysterious here – just realistic about the nature and difficulty of grasping certain important matters. Of course, he's a fierce advocate of thinking things through for yourself rather than getting your ethics unreflectively from traditional poetry.[52] There is no question of the depth of that commitment.

Russell: If you're right about that, why would he pull back right at the pinnacle of his account?

Jules: Because, as I said, he's being realistic. Although we can rule out some blind alleys with reason, disagreement about the most important things – including moral judgments – can and does go on indefinitely. Reason becomes a more powerful tool as judgment matures, along with a developed perceptivity about what matters most.

Alison: So Socrates concedes in many passages in the dialogues. It is part of why he insists on his ignorance. Important as it is, reason *alone* cannot replace tradition – or any other form of received knowledge – for figuring out how to live. Our education also needs certain kinds of stories. You will surely have noticed how frequently Socrates resorts to myths, tales, and allegories in his conversations.

---

52 In his *Preface to Plato*, Eric Havelock shows how the Socratic method of critical inquiry is a response to the widespread cultural practice in the ancient Aegean of treating the poets unreflectively as authoritative catalogues for almost every aspect of life, including morality. This history goes a long way toward explaining Plato's apparent hostility to art and poetry (in *Republic* II and III, and elsewhere). It thus may not be the arts as such that he views as dangerous, but rather the literal and uncritical ways his contemporaries use them.

Russell: I had noticed that, and simply assumed he was being inconsistent.

Jules: You surprise me, Russell, with this neglect of the principle of interpretive charity.[53] It never occurred to you that Socrates – the famous ironist – is being partly ironic, perhaps for a pedagogical purpose, when he exaggerates the importance of literal, discursive reason?

Russell: Frankly, it had not, but I'll bite. If it's not mystical, how is this "direct intellectual intuition" supposed to work?

Jules: I think we could be talking about something fairly mundane, something that even reason itself depends on. For example, could you write a simple argument on this napkin, listing the premises and conclusion?

Russell: Here you go. Any child could see its validity:
    1) All cats are vertebrates
    2) Samantha is a cat
Therefore
    3) Samantha is a vertebrate

Alison: I don't know, Russell. I'm not sure every child would be prepared to grasp the inference. If a child had a dog named Samantha, for example, she might challenge the second premise.

Russell: That would miss the point of the example. We're not talking about someone's dog, here, but Samantha the cat! And when we focus on the actual premises, we can clearly see that *if* they are true, the conclusion *must* be true.

---

53 The principle of interpretive charity involves a preparedness to give others the benefit of the doubt, interpreting their statements in the best possible light. To interpret charitably is not to read or listen uncritically, but rather involves a disinclination to condemn others' views except as a last resort. It is the practical basis for civility in discourse, as well as prerequisite for grasping unfamiliar texts and approaches.

Alison: Yes of course, but that's an exercise in abstraction that we have to learn. In some sense there's no *rational* way to show people that something is a reasonable inference. They just have to *see* that it is – the way we see embedded relationships in a diagram.

Jules: That is precisely the point I wanted to make, Alison, thank you. The conclusion follows the premises not merely as the third item on a list, but as a *consequence* of the first two, and one must experience that consequence for oneself in something resembling a tiny flash of insight. In this sense, I would argue, certain kinds of emotional experiences comprise the basis of reason itself.[54]

Russell: And as you hinted in your lecture, I suppose you think maturity is a core goal of learning, one which reason supports but cannot itself complete.

Jules: You read my mind, Russell. No doubt you've had students who are good at logic, able to spot fallacies wherever they occur and so forth, but who exhibit no restraint, or desire to understand difficult matters – they just like to show off and win verbal disputes. For these students the tools of logic are like machetes in the hands of toddlers.

Russell: I think I've had more than my fair share of those students. I don't really know what to do for them. Send them back to elementary school?

Alison: You may intend that snidely, Russell, but it could be just the sort of thing they do need, if what they should have received in their previous schooling was emotional nurturance and storytelling. I pursued graduate study in literature and poetry because I'm convinced even adults need stories at least as much as we need any other sort of knowledge.

---

[54] For a comic illustration of the refusal to accept an inference, see Lewis Carroll's famous dialogue "What the Tortoise Said to Achilles."

Jules: Here's a bit of logic for you Russell. First, stories are crucial to our maturation. Second, maturity is requisite for understanding. Third, feeling is the raw material of reason. It follows that Socrates is correct to use myths and tales in his teaching.

Stories, Feelings, Reason

Russell: I concede the obvious point that we couldn't reason if we didn't feel – we wouldn't even *bother* to reason if getting at the truth didn't matter to us. So emotive states like caring and desiring clearly precede and undergird logic. As Socrates himself observes, philosophy itself begins in wonder.[55]

Jules: If you'll come that far, Russell, I think you'll go the whole course. Take the concept of justice, one of Socrates' favorite examples. I contend, and I think Plato will back me up here, that we can't fully grasp the concept with reason alone.

Russell: I don't see why not. Our knowledge of justice may not be perfect, and could require revision as circumstances change, but we can reason our way to a pretty darn good idea of what is and is not just. Aside from the will to draw the relevant inferences, which I concede takes a certain degree of skill and courage, I fail to see the need for any wild emotional leaps.

Alison: You're right, we do have a pretty good idea of justice for most situations, Russell. But have you noticed that, whether as individuals, as nations, or as a species, we haven't implemented it very consistently?

Russell: When did you take up asking rhetorical questions, Alison?

---

[55] In reference to Plato's *Theatetus* 155D: "THEATETUS: [these problems] arouse my curiosity no end. Sometimes I get really dizzy from considering them. SOCRATES: ... this feeling – a sense of wonder – is perfectly proper to a philosopher: philosophy has no other foundation, in fact."

Alison: When did you? But if we understand justice well enough in principle, yet never seem to get around to acting on it, surely there is something incomplete in our understanding. We seem to get it discursively, but we don't fully feel it or live it. We might well call this a lack of judgment, or commitment, or maturity.

Russell: It just sounds like self-centeredness or greed to me.

Alison: That's my point, Russell. Someone who understands justice, and feels the normative force of that understanding, but is too self-centered to follow through, is precisely the sort of person who we say lacks judgment and maturity. Likewise, teachers who know their subjects, but lack patience and empathetic imagination to bring them alive for students, fail to enact principles of good teaching, even though they may be capable of reciting those principles.

Jules: This is simply Socrates' view that we don't *really* know something if we only grasp it intellectually but fail to act on it.[56]

Russell: Well, I always thought Aristotle got that one right, siding with common sense that we often do things even when we know they're wrong.[57] But I can see that there are two levels of knowing at issue here. Cognition by itself can be a rather anemic sort of knowing, if you don't act on what you know.

Jules: Yes, we complete our understanding by making it real. And a full *realization* of our learning goes beyond mere cognitive acknowledgment or words, bringing an idea bodily into being.

Russell: I wouldn't have put it that way myself, but thinking about the literal meaning of 'realization' perhaps goes some way to bridge the dispute between Plato and Aristotle.

---

[56] Plato's *Protagoras* 358 and elsewhere. An analogous argument in Plato's *Meno* 77C-78B concludes that everyone always aims at what is good – so the basic problem is an incomplete understanding of goodness.

[57] See Aristotle's *Nichomachean Ethics*, 1145b22.

Alison: In this context, something else I learned from Jules seems relevant: the root of *poiesia*, the source of our word 'poetry,' is the Greek verb for *making*. So we might well think of creative imagination as supplying a bridge between knowing something propositionally and realizing it in our lives.

Jules: These two levels of understanding map onto the distinction between knowing *that* and knowing *how*, in the sense of being materially and emotionally capable of enacting your knowledge. It was you, Russell, who suggested that we should collapse this distinction and construe all knowing as capability. In doing so, it seems, you concede Socrates' point.

Alison: You've caught Russell in his own net, Jules! Our purpose, however, is not to win but to learn – unless you're one of those toddlers with machetes! One feature of Socrates' method we might well emulate is always letting people change their minds in a discussion.[58]

Russell: It's entirely fair for you to move in for the kill on this one, Jules. As Aristotle points out, "Piety requires us to honor truth above our friends."[59] I grant that what the two of you are saying – along with Socrates – makes sense.

Alison: Our cleverness doesn't give us license to be barbarians, even when we're right. With all due respect to Aristotle, I think we really only honor truth if, *at the same time*, we also honor our friends.

Jules: Point taken, Alison. I didn't really mean to play "gotcha" with you, Russell. I get a little carried away in my enthusiasm sometimes.

---

58 E.g.: Plato's *Republic* I (340b).
59 Aristotle's *Metaphysics*, 1096a16.

Teaching and Deception

Russell: When you're right, you're right. Now let's see if you're right concerning your other misgivings about Socratic methods.

Jules: I alluded to one in my mini-lecture, what I take to be Socrates' capacity for disingenuity. Plato regularly has him present arguments that he *must* know are fallacious, and he seems to deceive and mislead his interlocutors repeatedly. I'm uncomfortable with the idea of a teacher being manipulative and untrustworthy.

Russell: This could be a real problem for the notion of Socrates as a pedagogical paragon. It is a long established principle that "… deception … is not a method or mode of teaching,"[60] and for some fairly obvious reasons.

Alison: Some of Socrates' lame arguments are obviously ironic jokes, not intended literally, so there's no deception. For example, at one point Socrates contends that we can find people with the contrary qualities needed to be guardians of a just city, at once spirited and contemplative. Puppies love those they know and hate those they don't, so are at once vigorous lovers of knowledge and haters of ignorance.[61]

Jules: But the character Glaucon accepts it, in that passage, with all apparent seriousness.

Alison: Maybe that's just because he grasps the larger point. The objection about contrary natures is a foolish quibble anyway, and deserves a joke for an answer. Socrates thereby anticipates and

---

[60] Israel Scheffler, *The Language of Education*, pp. 57-8. This passage occurs in the context of an observation that trying to teach something is not equivalent to getting the student to believe it by any means at all, but rather by helping the student to grasp the force of the reasons that support it.
[61] Plato's *Republic* II, 375d – 376b.

defuses potential quibbling later on. Approaching Plato's work as literature or dialogue rather than treatise dissolves many of these criticisms of his method.[62]

Russell: It would be quite a challenge to apply that sort of interpretation to all the dubious arguments in Plato, though it works for me in this case. But Jules's concern remains. If the Socratic teacher traffics in sophistic arguments and other manipulative tricks, should we really invite him into our classrooms?

Jules: That is precisely my question.

Alison: I don't know the answer, but it seems to me that one of us has to come to Socrates' defense. How about this, Jules? In claiming ignorance (*aporia*), Socrates is admitting to muddling through just like the rest of us. He has an idea of a useful direction to go, but doesn't claim to know for sure where he's going.

Jules: Yes, what of it?

Alison: If we could show that his use of dissimulation is, as you said, plausibly principled – aimed always at what the teacher takes to be the students' good – then perhaps it will appear no less, but also no more, problematic than the occasionally necessary use of paternalism that we were discussing earlier.

Russell: This might help. One measure of a flawed character, whether of a teacher or anyone else, is what lawyers call *mens rea*, or the guilty mind – deception with invidious intent.

Alison: I see where you're going, Russell. If the genuine intent is to educate rather than deceive, and deception is merely the necessary means…

---

62 See, e.g., Charles Griswold's anthology, *Platonic Writings, Platonic Readings*, for detailed analyses of how we might read Plato as literary dialogue.

Jules: So the end justifies the means?

Russell: What else do you suppose would justify them?

Jules: You miss the point. If the means themselves are morally dubious, a good end won't help – or reliably follow. Moreover, students must place a tremendous amount of trust in the teacher, and when this trust is betrayed with manipulation, you've undone the possibility of positive role modeling.

Alison: I think what Russell means is that an educator will use practically anything that works – grade consciousness, a bit of paternalist pressure, some clever misdirection – to see to it that the students get the education they deserve. I grant the legitimate concern about trust and betrayal, however, and I'm not sure how to deal with it.

Russell: Let's think a little bit about what sorts of things a principled teacher is likely to be strategically dishonest *about*. If we take seriously the notion of Socratic ignorance, *aporia*, then, many things a teacher presents are likely not to be true, or at least not completely true.

Alison: So the teacher's apparent dishonesty might arise from an honest limitation?

Russell: That, or an assessment of the *students'* limitations. Incomplete truths are all we really have, if we're honest with ourselves. I take it this is the root of Socrates' *aporia*. Socrates knows quite a lot, but he's being neither ironic nor disingenuous when he says he's ignorant. Part of being a teacher is developing a sense of how to present an array of incomplete truths productively.

Jules: But I take you to be sanctioning the presentation of truths we *know* to be incomplete, even when we ourselves actually have a *more* complete understanding.

Russell: Yes, I am, and I don't see anything wrong with that, so long as it seems necessary to bring the students along. I'm not even opposed to outright procedural deception. For example, I give a couple of quizzes early on in my introductory courses. I don't tell the students until later that these won't count toward their final scores.

Jules: That seems like a terrible way to build trust, and it will surely backfire when word gets out that it's your general practice.

Alison: He's a moving target in that respect, as I painfully recall from a logic course I took with him. Sometimes those quizzes don't count, and sometimes they do.

Jules: Russell snookered *you* with his early quiz trick?

Alison: He did, and I came to respect him for it, eventually. It motivated us to take the course seriously right from the start. Other students withdrew for fear of failure, but the rest of the class became a team, and we ended up having a lot of fun with logic.

Jules: To be charitable, I suppose you feel you must tell paternalistic lies like that when so many students are not serious about their learning. I also see how those attitudes can be a dead weight on everyone else's learning experience. Still, I don't like it, as it erodes trust.

Russell: This sort of paternalistic deception doesn't even necessarily betray trust, if students have a sophisticated enough grasp of the process – most kids figure out pretty early on that Santa Claus is imaginary, and quickly forgive their parents the playful fiction.[63]

---

[63] In *The Philosophical Baby*, Alison Gopnik observes that even very small children with imaginary friends generally understand that they are imaginary. When asked for details about them by an adult, "The children often interrupted to remind the interviewer, with a certain note of concern for her sanity, that these characters were, after all, just pretend – you know, not really *real*." (p. 53).

Alison: This is just the sort of thing I mean by the educational importance of literature and imagination, and again it helps to explain what Socrates is up to with his myths and tales. Given our ignorance, they may be necessary stepping stones to a fuller understanding of reality.[64]

Jules: But that seems very dangerous. The quiz thing is just sneaky, but very often a striking, though ultimately false, image sticks in a learner's head and obstructs further learning. Think how many people's understanding of physics and biology are permanently warped by simplistic images of atoms as miniature solar systems or DNA as beads on a string!

Alison: Say a little more about your second example, Jules. Is your point that an image like Watson's – DNA makes RNA, which in turn makes proteins that form phenotypic features – is so simple and appealing that it forms a dogmatic barrier to a richer and more realistic understanding?

Jules: Yes, and not only students get confused by it. Biologists have been culpably slow to see that genes can move around on chromosomes, and that the one-way, linear process sometimes operates in reverse, as with retroviruses. The simple, false story is so appealing that it's dangerous!

Russell: You've got a good point there. I'm inclined to think, though, that the problem begins with teachers who may not themselves understand the limits of their imagery – or the subjects they're teaching.

Alison: In that respect and others, it could just be bad storytelling.

---

64 In book II of Plato's *Republic*, Socrates and his conversants treat as unproblematic the common educational use of false tales: "Don't you understand, I said, "that first we tell tales [*mythoi*] to children? And surely they are, as a whole, false, though there are true things in them too." (377a). We might read this as a hint about Socrates' own procedure.

The history of our growing understanding of the mechanisms of inheritance is a fascinating one, from Mendel's peas to McClintock's jumping genes. If you told the whole story well, that little Mardi Gras-like image of beads on a string probably wouldn't undermine anyone's appreciation of genetics. It could even become a cautionary tale against scientific *hubris*.[65]

Jules: It has always been my contention that the only responsible way to teach any subject at all is with reference to its history, and these examples help to show why.[66] Learning is *discovery*, as Freire often said, and students who experience this through the narratives of their pedagogy are positioned to understand that we all have more to learn.

Russell: I like the idea that we place history at the core of our pedagogy. Just as students come to realize that the heroes of past learning turned out to be at best partially right, perhaps they will accept that their own teachers are caring and knowledgeable but limited, and that not everything we say is gospel.

Alison: I would hope they come to see precisely that – it is of the essence of critical thinking, after all, that we can dispassionately evaluate every source of information. I would also hope they come to see that even when we give them incomplete truths or useful fictions we aren't liars exactly, but Trickster-guides.

Teachers as Tricksters

Jules: I think I know what you mean by a trickster, Alison, but it's not entirely obvious to me why you capitalize the word.

---

[65] James Watson, co-discoverer of the structure of DNA and architect of the "central dogma" (his term) that DNA determines phenotype in a one-way, linear process, was famous throughout his career for no small measure of this human flaw.

[66] See Neil Postman, *The End of Education*.

Alison: Trickster is a sort of mythopoetic archetype. Folk tales from all over the world have characters who play Trickster roles: Coyote and Raven in native American tradition, Anansi the Spider in West Africa, the Mullah Nasrudin in south central Asia, Loki in Nordic mythology, and so on.

Russell: But why class Socrates with these fictional characters? After all, there really *was* a Socrates.

Alison: There may well have been a Mulla Nasrudin, too, a thirteenth century Sufi on whom the stories and jokes are based. We need to keep in mind Jules's insistence that our analysis speaks primarily of *Plato's character* Socrates, who may resemble the historical person in some respects but not others. For present purposes, it's the story that matters.

Jules: I did say that, but I was thinking of the way Plato emphasizes his relentless commitment to learning, remarkable memory, and focus on those with whom he speaks. I imagined these as probable exaggerations of the historical Socrates' actual qualities. This Trickster idea throws him into another level of literary invention.

Alison: The shift is not so huge, perhaps, if Plato's historical model had a light touch and a sense of humor – though we shouldn't underestimate Plato's capacity for subtle literary embellishment, either. In any case, if our image of an effective teacher is to contain a bit of Trickster, we might want a more realistic human model than some of those animal tales provide.

Russell: I'm sorry, and I don't mean to sound like a stuffy old literalist, but I'm not yet clear on the point of this Trickster idea, either for understanding Socrates, or for teaching.

Alison: Well, because Tricksters are marginal figures, operating on and pushing the borders of a society's self-understanding, they are often the disruptive and creative force that drives a society to re-evaluate and thus revitalize itself.[67]

Jules: I see that. Socrates uses terms like these at his trial when he likens himself to a horsefly annoying Athens and the Athenians so as to keep them alert and self-reflective.[68] In this respect and some others Socrates fits the image of a Trickster as well as anyone in world literature.

Alison: As an intellectual revolutionary, promoting critical thinking in place of traditional manly virtues, Socrates is very much on the creative, cutting edge of a society in crisis, and understandably he works mostly with the young – the locus of hope for any culture's future.

Russell: So teacher as Trickster is more than an explanation and justification for a certain sort of manipulation. Do you think Trickster-teachers play a critical role in the growth and revitalization of culture?

Alison: That's exactly what I think, and it stands on its head the conventional assumption that the main function of education is to indoctrinate students into the *status quo*. Though schools do help them learn how to function and succeed in the world as it is, education fails if it does not simultaneously raise serious questions about what the world could or should be.

Jules: I think that's another way of putting the point Freire makes about education and politics.

Russell: It well might be, but this way of framing the matter makes it a little more palatable to someone like me. Even a traditionalist

---

67 Lewis Hyde epitomizes this critical creative function in the title: *Trickster Makes This World; Mischief, Myth, and Art.*
68 Plato's *Apology*, 30E.

can respect the forces – including the creative and chaotic ones – that created tradition!

Jules: But I'm still a little uncomfortable with the deception involved. If as teachers we are in part Tricksters, I think it would behoove us always to *tell* the students that's what we're doing!

Alison: I don't have a problem with telling the students that I'm a Trickster-guide, if not necessarily in those terms. I always talk with my students about my methods – though occasionally only after the fact, where advance information would spoil the effect.

Jules: It's not at all clear to me that Socrates operates quite so openly as that in his manipulations.

Russell: An effective Trickster would have to be at least a *little* cagy. But now that you two have convinced me of the literary subtlety of Plato's writing, I will have to re-read it to see whether I think Socrates operates with a healthy balance of trickery and openness. As I think about it, I can remember at least a few passages where Socrates *does* telegraph his Trickster intentions…

Alison: Presumably our verdict on that will have to await a reconsideration of the dialogues. If it turns out that Socrates' manipulation doesn't live up to the principled standard we've identified, to that extent we will want to reject it as an admirable teaching technique.

Jules: That seems fair, but I have another concern. There's a darker side to the inegalitarianism of Socratic dialogues that many readers find troubling. So many of the responses from Socrates' interlocutors are perfunctory – of the "Yes, Oh, Socrates" sort – that it's hard not to think the dialogue form is something of a sham, and that Socrates is really just autocratically telling them what to think.

Alison: I felt that on first reading myself, and it is disturbing. It complicates my image of a Socratic conversation as a paradigm of an intellectual encounter among equals.

Russell: Now it's my turn to defend Socrates. I think that paradigm may be no more than an anachronistic projection. In most of the dialogues, Socrates' conversants are not in any sense his equals, and the text gives no indication that they should be.

Jules: I'd say that's true of most of the so-called early and middle dialogues, and some of the later ones as well. Even in those that might be exceptions, like *Gorgias*, Socrates ends up speaking most of the time not with Gorgias himself, but with his student Polos, whom Plato presents as young and impulsive.[69]

Alison: Interesting. One way we could interpret this is as an emphasis on Socrates as a teacher – and it is mostly the young and less experienced who are prepared to subject themselves to learning.

Russell: That phrase "subject themselves" is telling. Socrates is in many senses not a traditional teacher. He says at his trial that he doesn't charge fees or claim to be able to impart any particular subject matter, and he certainly has no institutional authority to evaluate students' performance. Nonetheless, he commands respect, and the young men are right to defer to him.

Jules: I know you don't have a problem with the old teacher-as-authority-figure notion, Russell, but I certainly do, for some of the reasons we have discussed already.

---

69 At one point, Socrates even puns on Polos' name, which is Greek for 'colt,' as a comment on his behavior (463E). We might read this passage as a transparent example of Socratic Tricksterism.

Russell: You may find it ideologically distasteful, but in my view a teacher must both have and exercise some kind of authority to be effective – and it had better not be arbitrary.

Jules: How could it be otherwise?

Russell: Precisely by *grounding* its paternalism. Notice the narrative arc of a typical Socratic dialogue. First Socrates convinces his interlocutors that they, like himself, are ignorant in the aporetic sense. Once he has established his authority and secured their willingness to learn, he can then guide them through a genuinely philosophical search. He is able to do this only because he has taken charge.[70]

Alison: I agree with you to a point, Russell. Socrates dominates the discussion, though he somehow manages to do so without being domineering. He has a pretty light touch most of the time. I think this is partly because the young men *choose* to be present, and to continue the conversation. When they say they agree, they presumably do so of their own free will. Perhaps it is only the brevity of the writing that makes "Yes, Oh Socrates" seem slavish.

Russell: And don't forget, as Jules pointed out, they are always free to change their minds about anything they previously agreed to.

Alison: Yes, and when they do resist, change their minds, or question the direction of the dialogue, Socrates pays attention and redirects it in response.[71]

---

70 For example, it is plausible to interpret much of Book I of *Republic* as a process of Socrates wresting attention and authority from both Cephalos, the head of the family, and Thrasymachos, a famous sophist, as preparation for leading the rest of the conversation.

71 In one striking example, only after cajoling and insistence by the entire party at the beginning of *Republic* V does Socrates undertake to address the suitability of women to serve as guardians in his imaginary city. It is fair to say that he deliberately, and Trickster-like, provokes this demand with a seemingly offhand comment about the "commonality of women and children" in Book IV (423E).

Jules: That's true, though in many cases he may have manipulated them into asking certain questions or pursuing particular issues, so the conversation takes the course he really wants it to after all, while merely *appearing* to be responsive to the others' interests.

Russell: But that's the genius of it! Even if Socrates is playing his friends, and is being ironic with his protestations that it is they, not he, who insist on a certain topic, it is still *their* interests and concerns that drive the discussion.

Alison: …because if they *think* they are curious about something, it follows that in some meaningful sense they really *are* curious about it, even if Socrates covertly provoked the question?

Russell: Precisely. You two have convinced me that Socrates' authority as a teacher derives from his cleverness as a principled Trickster, and his brand of trick can be a very effective teaching method – maybe the best.

Alison: This has gotten me thinking, too. Very young children learn, and learn voraciously through play, without realizing they're studying. Preschool teachers can structure play so that it orders and instructs while seeming merely fun. And anyone who could charm older students or direct their curiosity through play would be a very effective teacher.

Jules: Somehow I'm less uncomfortable with either teacherly authority or manipulation wielded in a playful fashion. Is that what Socrates is really doing?

Alison: That again is a question we could only settle with a careful re-reading of Plato – and no way of reading him could be entirely wrong if it drives us to read him again![72] Maybe promoting this sort of critical re-reading, is what our Authors intended, by both the question mark and by the term 'New' in their heading.

---

[72] Sayre, *Plato's Literary Garden*, p. xi.

Russell: Of course, a *critically re-examined* Socratism seems very much in the spirit of Socrates himself. But please, don't start in on that theological business about Authors again!

Interlude

Russell Steadman

As I said, my interest in teaching was born late and not without a little pain. Though I have come to appreciate teaching's rare joys and victories, I also know that most battles never stay entirely won. Philosophy is a bit like that, too: after long effort one gains insight into some question, and experiences a sparkling moment of satisfaction, only to discover a fresh argument or a wider context that problematizes the matter once again. At least with scholarship, though, I can pursue this process at my own pace, hanging on to my apparent solutions until I feel ready to rethink them. Teaching can be infuriatingly Heraclitean – no answer to a pedagogical problem, however elegant, affects students in the same way twice.

I don't mean to sound like a recluse or curmudgeon retreating into his ivory silo. I'm well aware that life is messy, that anything really worth accomplishing involves an unending struggle. But I'm approaching retirement age, and I find to my great frustration that I have less and less in common with my students each year. To engage in philosophy together, beyond the potent but dry analytical tools of formal logic, we require a rich common culture of experiences, images, literary and artistic references, and a shared appreciation for the wonder of it all, not to mention a willingness to discuss and disagree about it. I have become who I am thanks to books, music, theater, and living culture of all sorts – the immense privilege of growing up surrounded by a great university in a time of uprising and ferment. Yet very little of this means anything to most of my students, who do not read or participate in political action, and each of whom has his or her own earbudded microculture, largely obscure to everyone else. Absent these connections, I'm often pressed to be even more authoritarian than I already am. We become what we pretend to be, and I don't much care for the angry disciplinarian who too often follows me home after a day in the classroom. I think maybe, with considerable regret, it may be time to hang up the spurs.

So with my own children grown, I'm beginning to imagine retirement from teaching. Not to move to Florida and play golf, heaven forbid, but to devote myself to various philosophical projects for which I have never found the time, to get a little more serious about my gardening, and perhaps at long last take up a musical instrument. And in tribute to my father, I'd like someday to fix up an old steam engine and give kids rides through the town park – if kids these days still enjoy that sort of thing.

Chapter Six

Between Content and Character

How do we balance teaching objective content while encouraging students' autonomous development into mature learners? Is character development a necessary concomitant to effective teaching? How are intellectual virtues like interpretative charity and passion for truth related to moral character?

Russell: I'm curious, and frankly a little troubled, by the earlier suggestion that character development is at the heart of learning, and perhaps even more important than reasoning itself.

Alison: It was Jules who raised that point, I think. Since I don't normally associate you with social conservatism, Jules, when you and Plato suggest that the development of character is a central aim of education, I have to think you mean something different from the "values education" some conservatives embrace as their mantra.

Jules: I would be as surprised as you to find myself in such company, but it would be churlish to assume automatically that my view has nothing in common with theirs. First we have to figure out what I actually have in mind!

Socratic "Values Education"?

Alison: I think our reasoning in the last chapter amounted to something like this: if we are as honest with ourselves as Socrates, we realize that we lack any final knowledge of the most important things, including what is good, beautiful, just, and so on. In this state of ignorance our reasoning, however proficient, relies for its premises on probabilities and likely stories at best.

Jules: That's right. To use Plato's picture of our state of learning, we are groping about in a darkened cave.[73] So, as indispensable as critical thinking is, it can at most lay the groundwork for good judgment and the will to live consistently with its conclusions. Given the incompleteness of our knowledge, what we most need to learn is character – kindness, generosity, patience, empathy, and so forth.

Russell: Well, you are assuming Plato's theories are correct, that universal Forms or Ideas are the source of being and knowability for the perceivable world. What I think, instead, is that we know many things, however fallibly, and should devote our energies to teaching them, rather than mucking about in students' characters.

Jules: Remember that Plato himself never speaks in his dialogues, and claims in the *Seventh Letter* that he has not and never would commit his theories to writing, since language itself is utterly unsuited as a medium for philosophy.[74] So I don't think we can assume that even Plato subscribes to the theory of forms, except as an intellectual challenge for his characters.[75] Moreover, I think

---

[73] *Republic* VII, 514c-517a. "…make an image of our nature in its education and want of education…see human beings as though they were in an underground cave…"

[74] *Seventh Letter*, 341C.

[75] Plato's later dialogues (*Theatetus, Sophist, Statesman,* etc.) seem not to employ the theory in any doctrinaire fashion, and the *Parmenides* critiques it devastatingly.

Plato's disclaimer hints that real learning is deeper than language – in short, a matter of character.

Alison: Perhaps our considered view will be independent of how we interpret Plato's theories of knowing and being. We agree that we *are* ignorant of some of the most important things in our lives. I'm not suggesting that we understand nothing at all about them; we're simply lacking the will or capacity to bring them to full realization. Even without the theory of Forms, an acknowledgement of fallibility seems to entail the necessity of character development.

Jules: And this being so, I don't see how we can avoid placing character – what Socrates himself might have called the ongoing attempt to know oneself – at the core of learning and teaching.

Russell: Fair enough, but I still say this argument relies too heavily on debatable theories about the very nature of Plato's project.

Character and Intellectual Virtues

Jules: Okay, let me offer an alternative argument for this insight about character, based on some of your own observations. You said earlier that learning is challenging because it involves a change in the learner him or herself, which is almost always emotionally difficult.

Russell: I said something of the sort, yes. What of it?

Jules: From your psychological insight it follows that the effort to learn – even when the content is no more directly concerned with morality than a multiplication table or an A-major scale – both *engages* the learner's identity and *alters* it.

Alison: I can accept that as a curiosity, Jules, but I don't yet see where you're going with it.

Jules: If we are right about this identity-involvement in learning, it follows that we constantly re-configure our personal commitments in the learning process, no matter what we learn. This means that in some sense our basic values, commitments, judgments – one might even metaphorically say our souls – are at stake in our every learning moment.

Alison: That's an interesting argument. It follows that it would be both foolish and dangerous to pretend – especially in a school or university setting where we claim to have a good idea both what is worth learning and how best to teach it – that we can concern ourselves solely with the *content* of learning to the exclusion of the *process*. If you're right, it's all about moral engagement, however we slice it.

Russell: That is cogent so far as it goes, but can or should we concern ourselves with the moral aspects of our students' lives? More to the point, is it our responsibility? Suppose you, Alison, taught a brilliant student to play the piano, and this student went on to become a successful and innovative musician, but also an international jewel thief. I think you can fairly share credit for the one, but not responsibility for the other.

Jules: That's a pretty extreme example!

Russell: It's unrealistic, I admit, but I only mean to heighten the contrast.

Alison: I accept that unbalanced characters exist, if perhaps more frequently in fiction and on television than in life. More common are less dramatically bifurcated people, good at their work but neglectful of their families, for example. But isn't it hard to escape the thought that something is lacking in their educations, if they haven't learned to maintain a healthy balance?

Jules: Balance itself is an example of a moral lesson we get with every discipline, not just gymnastics, and we rightly also admire people who exhibit what we call *integrity*. Literally and etymologically, integrity is a healthy, dynamic integration of the parts of the self, though in everyday conversation we tend to confine it to a narrow moral metaphor. But you can't be a good student *or* a good person without it.

Alison: Surely you will concede, Russell, that you teach for integrity as well as, say, logical ability? In fact, I doubt if students could even succeed in one of your logic courses without cultivating a number of fairly robust virtues – intellectual integrity and honesty, a passion for truth, humility, interpretive charity, and so forth.

Russell: Those are, as you say, *intellectual* virtues, as distinct from moral ones.

Jules: Distinct conceptually, I agree, but very hard to separate in practice. I submit that when you demonstrate the principle of interpretive charity for your students, for example, and expect them to make it habitual, you are exercising their moral muscles along with their logical ones. Even the act of en*courag*ing your students seems to contain the moral concept of *courage*...

Russell: Let's dial that down a notch, Jules. Etymology is a useful tool for grasping the sources of words, but if we let it dictate all meaning, we poor English speakers would be left speaking mainly ancient Latin, Greek or Sanskrit – and saying nothing new even in those languages!

Jules: I concede that the link between encouragement and courage is only suggestive. But etymology aside, think about how you choose to present intellectual virtues in teaching critical thinking. I notice that you admit in your own syllabi that it's not enough to memorize a list of skills. You insist that students adopt them as *habits* and *dispositions*!

Russell: We call intellectual virtues those abilities and dispositions of mind that tend to foster understanding and avoid errors in thinking. It could perhaps be that practicing them might dispose a person to acquire corresponding moral habits as well. Interpretive charity is enough *like* moral concern, and intellectual humility like the other kind, that one might well pick up some of one from practicing the other.

Jules: That's enough of a concession for me, Russell. I'm inclined to go further and say that students are unlikely to be fully accomplished in reasoning without it being integral to the rest of their lives, including their moral characters, but your concession of an analogical relationship is sufficient.

Russell: Sufficient for what?

Jules: To show that, in fact, we *do* understand something about how to shape students' characters, and that it's inseparable from the content we're teaching them.

Alison: I'm quite moved by your reasoning, Jules. Let me say something in light of it about Russell's jewel-thief musician example. Music is apparently the most literally integrative human activity, in terms of its effects on the brain.[76] Thus if my piano student did become a jewel thief, I suspect – and sincerely hope – it would not merely be *independent* of her training, but actively *despite* it.

Indoctrination and Reason

Russell: Okay, you two win. Suppose we say, for the sake of discussion, that all learning is in some sense moral, involving

---

[76] See Daniel J. Levitin, *This is Your Brain on Music*.

character development. How will we go about teaching it? As Alison has observed, we can't imagine you indoctrinating children with right-wing dogma, Jules, and based on what we agreed in our conversation about Freirean pedagogy, I would expect you to reject liberal or leftist indoctrination as well.

Jules: You're right, Russell, and that's where I part company with the conservative wing of the "values education" crowd. In the first place such proposals tend toward reductive individualism, whereas I view the development of character as deeply rooted in social conscience – it's all about *relationship*. Moreover, dogmatic attempts to program young people's views on hot-button moral issues are not only inconsistent with other educational values we have identified – respecting students' autonomy, for example – but they tend to backfire.

Alison: In the long run you may be right that natural rebellious impulses will work against attempts to regiment students' values and intuitions, but the short run can be pretty nasty, too.

Russell: It certainly can. Think of the Chinese youth mobilized as Red Guards by Mao Zedong in the late 1960s. The movement took demagogic bullying to new heights in inculcating certain "revolutionary" values, and was so successful it murdered thousands, blighted a generation, and almost spawned civil war.[77]

Jules: As I said, moral indoctrination tends to backfire, one way or another.

Alison: But since it can be horrifically destructive in the process, we need a better argument against it than that. Telling young people what to think and do is a perennial temptation and a great danger, however they act on it.

---

[77] See Andrew G. Walder's *Fractured Rebellion: The Beijing Red Guard Movement*.

Russell: That it is. Fortunately, we can simply provide them with the foundational principles of learning – critical thinking, autonomy, and so forth – and turn them loose.

Jules: There's nothing simple about it, I think. We seem to have returned to the question of the neutrality of rational tools. But notice: you just agreed that good habits of thought – those likely to yield knowledge and avoid error – are at least analogous to moral virtues, and earlier you admitted that immoderate use of logical tools can empower students in frightening ways. Watch out for toddlers with machetes!

Alison: You do seem to have boxed yourself into a corner, Russell. We may have discovered that, however uncomfortable we are with the prospect, our students' character must be our business.

Russell: With some reluctance, I suppose I have to grant the point.

Jules: Turnabout is fair play. I tentatively allowed a little while ago that that the values we've been discussing – critical thinking, autonomy, and so forth – are not partisan alternatives but foundational principles, propaedeutic to exploring and adopting any particular views, and themselves subject to critique. And the more we think about it, the less tentative I feel.

Russell: If you're wholeheartedly behind that proposition, I guess I can give some ground on this one.

Alison: Even our bedrock principles are always open for further discussion, though I'm inclined to think we're right about these two. I think we're also right to be against indoctrination and dogma, and we also seem to be on the same page, for at least practical reasons, regarding the problems with teaching character *directly* – the old Victorian idea of inculcating moral lessons by direct prescription and threat, still so popular with some moral conservatives.[78]

Russell: As the token conservative in this discussion, though no fan of bullying dogma, I want to give this devil his due a little longer. We know, for example, that it's wrong to hit others, and that hitting solves nothing. This is both a foundational moral principle and an empirical finding of developmental psychology. Not hitting is a good and – intellectually if not in practice – a non-controversial value. What could be wrong with simply imposing it as a rule, dogmatically and paternalistically if you like, on students of all ages?

Alison: And how exactly will we enforce this rule? By threatening corporal punishment?

Jules: Alison's question is reasonable. Young people have acute noses for hypocrisy, and our society's propensity for continual warfare, coupled with an entertainment culture that glorifies violence and magnifies its prevalence, makes such a strategy implausible. We might succeed in *suppressing* hitting in school that way, but we won't be teaching character.

Alison: So what would it take to teach character, supposing for example that our target trait was non-violence?

Jules: Well, I don't know, but at the very least it seems like we would have to engage them, age-appropriately, in reasoned discourse about the matter.

---

78 After leaving public office, former U.S. Secretary of Education William J. Bennett published a series of best-selling books of moral instruction and dogma, mirroring popular 19th century cautionary tales for children. Their unapologetic prescriptivness and lack of moral complexity earned him the unofficial title "national scold."

Russell: I'm glad to see we've got you on board with the discursive engagement element, Jules. I'd have to say that's not likely to be enough in this case, though, given the deep emotional level on which violence moves people. I'm afraid we will need to engage students' *feelings* about violence, somehow, at a visceral level. And I honestly don't know how to do that.

Narrative Imagination and Felt Reasons

Alison: I think I do. One of the reasons I enjoy teaching literature is that it stimulates our capacity for empathetic imagination. When interesting characters in a story well told feel the force of something, whether an argument or an explosion, readers vicariously feel it as well, and thereby get an inkling of how to process those experiences. This helps them to imagine alternative emotional responses to events in their own lives.

Russell: Come to think of it, there's some discussion of this in the literature on teaching critical thinking. Siegel, for example, talks about the power of a Dostoyevsky novel to bring reasoning to life – to bring us face to face with "felt reasons," as I think he calls them.[79]

Alison: Yes, I've read that essay, and I think it's a good start. If reasoning is more than a mere hobby or abstract mental exercise, we must come to *feel* the probative force of reasons as motives for both belief and action. Fully to learn to *reason*, then, we must educate our capacity to *feel*.

Jules: This suggestion erodes further the alleged distinction between knowing and doing. If you're right that a proper understanding of reasons entails not just drawing their propositional conclusions but feeling their force and acting accordingly, then we can only

---

79 Siegel, "Teaching, Reasoning, and Dostoyevsky's *The Brothers Karamazov*" in *Rationality Redeemed?*

understand either knowing or doing properly as an extension of the other.

Russell: That's helpful, Jules. But Alison, why do you say Siegel's piece is no more than a good start?

Alison: The point he makes is clear enough, but our purpose is wider. You asked how we can teach character, and Jules suggests that making students memorize virtues or telling them what values to adopt is foolish, ineffective, dangerous, or all three. My proposal is that we approach the teaching of character indirectly, by engaging the free play of imagination.

Russell: I see. You think Siegel's focus on using literature to learn how to feel *reasons* is only part of the equation.

Alison: Exactly. There are other things one must learn how to feel before one can decide what sort of person to become. One's characterological choices need to be richly informed – aesthetically and morally as well as cognitively.

Jules: So maybe teaching even well-founded values and character directly – as though they were multiplication tables – is problematic and ineffective because it undermines a student's autonomy precisely at its most critical undertaking.[80]

Alison: I would say so. The central reason schools should be radically unlike factories is that their raw materials as well as their products are *persons*. Even when we're shoveling in data like multiplication tables or running quality control protocols we need to remind ourselves of this.

---

80 In Tobias Wolff's *Old School*, Mr. Ramsey, a teacher at at a preparatory high school, rails against the cloying pieties of an "honor code": "Strange word, honor – can't be spoken aloud, turns immediately to bilge… Make good rules and hold the boys to them. No need to be pawing at their souls. Honor Code? Pretentious nonsense," p. 149.

Jules: Doesn't Whitehead say something along these lines as well, Alison?

Alison: *That's* an observation worthy of memorization, and I carry it with me as a talisman:

> ...students are alive, and the purpose of education is to stimulate and guide self-development. It follows as a corollary from this premise, that the teachers also should be alive with living thoughts.[81]

Russell: This is certainly something you embody in your work, Alison.

Jules: I can attest to that as well. But if he's listening, your devil will no doubt agree with me, Russell, that what I propose in values or character education is not simply a left-wing mirror of conservative dogmatism, but rather an insistence on the basic epistemic and social ground rules for growth and inquiry.

Russell: As I said, I recognize that very clearly. The sorts of value we inculcate when we teach reasoning skills or intellectual virtues are, in my view, independent of any spectrum of ideological opinion. This is precisely what I was trying to get at earlier when I defended the neutrality of reason.[82]

Alison: I think we may treat that as established, at least among ourselves.

Jules: But Alison, can you say more for us about how stories work for you in the classroom? Maybe you could give us a mini-lecture about your techniques.

---

[81] Alfred North Whitehead, *The Aims of Education*, p. v.
[82] In Chapter Three

Alison: I'm all through attempting formal lectures, thank you, but I will tell you an interesting story about a former student. Let's call him Nick. This isn't an example of teaching moral imagination through literature, if that's what you were hoping for, but I think the story illustrates how closely character development adheres to learning, and how we teachers must struggle with that.

> Nick was bright, with great verbal facility and a sharp mind. I never had to encourage him to speak up. On the contrary, I once or twice took him aside to enlist his assistance in drawing out the other students. You could call this a Trickster-like ruse, designed at once to prevent him from dominating the class discussion, and at the same time to shift the source of encouragement away from the teacher. I find students can generally hear things from their peers that fall on deaf ears from an authority. I can't claim the strategy was terribly effective in this instance, but it may have helped some.
>
> I also strongly suggested to Nick that, before speaking up in class, he jot down questions and comments that occur to him, in order to open a reflective space in which he could make choices about what to bring up. This also met with mixed success. Nick was something of a force of nature, and for much of the term I had serious doubts whether I could teach him or, though this might sound presumptuous, whether he was at all teach*able*. He was like a talented and promising young athlete, a natural, who finds enough success with his own reflexes and enthusiasm that he never develops the skill of heeding a coach's advice. Failing a sudden burst of maturation, I could imagine him becoming one of Jules's toddlers with machetes.
>
> The athletic analogy seems apt when I remember a conversation we had early in the course about the role discourse and cognitive analysis play in learning a physical skill. Nick had been a competitive swimmer at one time, and he recalled that

when he listened to his coach and began *thinking* about how he moved his limbs, rather than just doing it, he found that it slowed him down. Other students with analogous experiences observed that this commonly happens, for a time, but that with practice an athlete can assimilate the altered technique, and eventually improve substantially on the earlier performance. I caught a look on Nick's face, at once quizzical and skeptical, that made me think perhaps he had not gone far enough to experience this process for himself, and was hearing the thought for the first time. Only much later did it occur to me that his failure to experience that breakthrough in swimming might be emblematic of his approach to learning in general.

One day fairly late in the semester the class happened upon the subject of verbal competitiveness, and whether it tends to stimulate or inhibit learning. Nick, as the most competitive student in the class, was of course in favor, reasoning that, as in a judicial proceeding, the truth would be most likely to emerge from each side making its most vigorous, adversarial case. Another student objected that such a procedure seemed better suited to produce definite winners and losers of a verbal battle than to discover the truth of the matter, which we might better pursue collaboratively. In partial support of this latter claim, I suggested to Nick that his regular impulse to pipe up "I disagree" in response to statements of the other students or myself might not be the most fruitful rhetorical strategy, inspiring more defensiveness than curiosity. I proposed some alternative responses, such as "Interesting that it seems so to you," "I wonder whether it's true," and the like. As with my earlier strategy, I was hoping to harness Nick's mental facility for more thoughtful, less reactive conversation.

The course had an online forum for discussion beyond the class meetings, and this question of adversarial style generated lively and thoughtful exchanges, giving me an opportunity to mention a Socratic dialogue we had read in class which highlights the distinction between a philosophical discussion, where we all do our best to figure out together what's the case, and a sophistical one, where the motives are displaying cleverness and claiming victory. After this topic ran its course, I noticed that Nick was considerably subdued during several subsequent class meetings. I had no idea of the source of this unaccustomed reticence, but I got a clue in his written course evaluation later on. In answer to the question "What was the most unexpected aspect of the course for you?" he wrote in part: "I've never been criticized for arguing adversarially before, so that was the most unexpected aspect. Thank you for that." His mention of this issue, and especially the thanks appended to it, suggest to me not only that my worries about Nick's educability were unfounded, but that in the matter of character specifically, where in my perception he most needed work, all is not lost.

Russell: That's a wonderful story, Alison. Of course, as in most teaching you will probably never know what comes of it, but there are grounds for hope that Nick might really grow as a person because of the experience. It is interesting that he interpreted your suggestions as criticism. It's characteristic of youth to take these things personally.

Alison: He had good enough reasons, aside from youth, to take them on as personal challenges. If I had a lighter touch as a teacher I might perhaps have conveyed the lesson more subtly, but I was struggling, and a little frustrated myself at the time.

Jules: I am shocked, *shocked*, to hear you admit that teachers, including even yourself, are human!

Russell: All joking aside, it occurs to me to speculate that one reason standardized or high-stakes tests are poor predictors of anything is that character development is so idiosyncratic, non-uniform, and thus hard to test for.

Alison: That insight could be independent confirmation of our thesis that intangibles of this kind are at the heart of learning.

Educational Competition?

Jules: If so, I would welcome such confirmation. But the issue of competitiveness your story mentions is one that intrigues me. Many of my best students have intense competitive streaks. I can see that it is a large piece of their motivation, but it makes me very uncomfortable.

Russell: It shouldn't, Jules. That sort of youthful spiritedness is just what we need more of. It enlivens the classroom, and it's one of the few prominent sources of internal motivation available. It enhances those precious pedagogical relationships you think are so important. I say bring it on!

Jules: Okay, Russell, you win.

Russell: Don't be silly. We haven't even started to dispute it!

Jules: That's my point. Many students don't care to compete, and quickly give up when it starts to seem like a race. In many ways they're right to do so, since learning is *not* a race, but a cooperative search for understanding.

Alison: I don't want to sound like a tape loop, but it's becoming pretty clear that my role in this conversation is to point out over and over again that you're both right. A certain amount of good-natured competition, as between you two cowboys, can indeed stimulate creative thought and learning, and it can energize a dialogue and sharply clarify issues – as it often does for us.

Jules: So far it sounds like you agree with Russell. How is it you think we're both right?

Alison: I intend my qualifiers "a certain amount" and "good-natured" to acknowledge the force of your analysis, Jules. We seemed to have struck on one characterological issue central to all pedagogy – that becoming a collaborative learner involves being just a little disputatious, but at the right time and in the right spirit.

Russell: But Alison, "getting a feel" for something like that is a constantly moving target. It changes with the topic, the individuals in the class, even the time of day or the mood of the moment. How can I be responsible for all of that and the subject-matter, too?

Alison: It's not easy, but negotiating labyrinths of interpersonal variables is, I'm afraid, precisely what we sign up for when we become teachers.

Russell: Makes me almost wish for the good old days when I thought I only had to know my discipline!

Alison: Perhaps we should distinguish different sorts of competitiveness. When the primary goal is to dominate and humiliate others, competition can play no useful role in the learning process, and can actually destroy it. However, there is nothing wrong with a healthy spiritedness among learners, cheerfully vying with one another to come up with useful contributions.

Jules: It seems to me that it would be easier if we could exclude competitiveness from the classroom altogether. I'll appeal again to Plato: Socratic philosophical inquiry seeks understanding for its own sake, whereas disputation is sophistic and anti-philosophic, seeking only victory or personal point-scoring.

Alison: Banishing competition might well *seem* easier, but Russell is correct that for many students competing with each other, or with the teacher, is a major source of what motivates them to pursue understanding. It may not be precisely the slow burn of balanced, sensitive curiosity we might wish for, but it has the virtue of being internal in a strong sense, so it mimics the sort of motivation we need to cultivate.

Jules: You're suggesting the trick would be to *use* the force of competitive impulse, but moderate it and turn it subtly toward a nobler and more cooperative purpose – a sort of social and intellectual *jiu-jitsu*?[83]

Alison: I have in mind just such a Trickster-like approach. One way to start is to discuss with your students, early in a course, explicit guidelines for how you and they will conduct respectful class discussion. Within the boundaries of civility, cultivated listening habits, and overt expressions of respect for those with whom one disagrees, a good-natured dispute can be an effective and inclusive experience.

Jules: That sort of thing won't even seem like real competition to those with a fierce combative spirit.

Alison: It might not, but get those students competing with one another for how gracious and respectful they can be, and see how quickly the ego-motive will erode the sand out from under its own feet!

Russell: Well, when you lay it out like that, helping students understand how to be mildly disputatious without being obstreperous doesn't sound quite so daunting.

---

[83] Jules presumably intends this term in its popular, metaphorical sense of overcoming larger or stronger opponents by turning their own strength against them, rather than any technical reference to a specific martial art.

Interlude

Alison Bridges

I have always kept up my musical interests. Surprising as it sounds, I find an hour or two playing Chopin preludes or tunes from the Great American Songbook on my baby grand intensely relaxing after a day's teaching – and before an evening's stack of student writing and lesson plans. I used to play with a community orchestra, but some friends and I started a jazz ensemble a couple years ago, and now we play weekend gigs in area restaurants and at summer garden parties. I have never understood how people can like only one kind of music, as I find something powerful in all of it, and in particular the rich traditions of jazz and classical piano inform and inspire each other endlessly for me.

Making a living with music, though, is not something I had never seriously imagined, but a recent invitation to audition for the Pioneer Valley Symphony Orchestra caught me off guard. I have no idea whether I could really get the job, but even the abstract possibility hit me like a thunderbolt. Could I really imagine giving up teaching? I grant all the problems with the schools, testing, and cultural barriers to real learning, and I feel all of the challenges and exhaustion that drive so many of us away, but I do so love the flash of discovery in the eyes of a young person, and sometimes I think there are too few of us prepared to stand aside and let that light shine out.

Conclusion

Bridges to the Reader

Reader: Hello, Alison! I wondered whether I'd find the three of you here. I was just sitting at the other end of the Bridge of Flowers reading through the last chapter. I hope you don't mind the intrusion, but I've got a few questions.

Alison: That's great. Jules, Russell, I would like you to meet our reader and benefactor.

Russell: Benefactor? I haven't seen any royalties yet!

Jules: It's a pleasure to meet you. Our only real profit, like that of most teachers, is merely to be known and understood and, when we are lucky, a positive force in the lives of our students.

Reader: I'd be willing to bet that your frequent success is more than just good luck. In fact, I feel as though I know you all quite well by this point, even though I've only briefly spoken with Alison. As for understanding – as I said I've got some questions. If the three of you can hold any more coffee, please let me buy you some and pick your brains.

Jules: See, Russell? The ink is barely dry and already you're in for a free cup of coffee! Make mine a green tea, please.

Russell: Just kidding about the royalties, of course. As a terminal academic, I know better than to hope for financial profits from my scholarship. But I won't say no to coffee.

Alison: Nor will I. So, what puzzles can we clear up for you?

What's a Paradox?

Reader: I'm still a little confused about the way you use the idea of paradox. It's a central theme of your whole conversation, but I don't recall you saying exactly what you mean by it.

Russell: I think I can help you there. Paradox has technical meanings in logic and mathematics, but we're employing it more colloquially, to refer to certain kinds of conceptual tensions among ideas or goals.[84] A paradox of this sort can be anything that sets up cognitive dissonance, say between the educational goal of autonomy and the paternalist means by which we seek to realize that goal.

Jules: More specifically, the paradoxes we discuss here are the kinds of practical pedagogical puzzles that seem at first insoluble, but on reflection turn out to have good solution strategies. However, as effective as these strategies are in negotiating the contradictions, they turn out not quite to be complete solutions, and we find we must tackle the puzzles all over again when we encounter a different class, a new student, or steep spot on a learning curve.

---

84 Etymologically, paradox suggests a surprising comparison with received opinion or appearance. Thus a statement is paradoxical that seems contradictory on its face, contradicts a common assumption, or is true despite appearing false or incoherent. In this dialogue the emphasis is not so much on single statements as such, but on tensions within the complex states of affairs we encounter in teaching and learning.

Alison: You may have recognized this kind of paradox, when having to improvise your way through any unexpected turn in your professional or personal life.

Reader: Well, yes, and that's clarifying, but why didn't you say something about it earlier on?

Alison: We did mention it in passing, I think, but paradox is an open-ended notion with several meanings, and we thought perhaps it was best just to let it simmer for awhile. Also, I find the best time to answer a question is after, rather than before, we have piqued your curiosity.

Reader: Well, I would have asked earlier if I'd had a chance.

Alison: I'm sorry about that. What else would you have asked earlier?

Is Dialogue Really Philosophy?

Reader: Well, I'm puzzled by the way the conversation moves around, never staying focused on a single issue or paradox for very long, but circling back and following tangents.

Alison: Isn't that the way most conversations go?

Reader: Yes, I suppose it is, but in picking up a book on the philosophy of education I expected something more systematic.

Russell: I'm with you. I like nothing better than an essay that lays out its reasoning in rigid logical form, defines its terms systematically, and makes its case in the smallest possible number of pages. Of course, that kind of writing places severe demands on a non-specialist's patience, and necessarily relies on lots of technical jargon.

Jules: To those limitations I would add that specialized monographs not only fail to speak to the ordinary reader, they sometimes can fail to address real-world concerns – and I admit this as someone with scientific training. The severe reduction in scope necessary to think and write in a formal style too often generates a sort of tunnel vision, buying clarity at the expense of applicability.

Alison: But our conversational approach to philosophical problems in education is hardly an attempt to sugar-coat difficult ideas, much less water them down. On the contrary, I have found this kind of discourse to be a powerful method, in the spirit of Socrates, for any kind of philosophical inquiry. Some rigorous meandering has virtue, I think.

Reader: So you're saying you hope to figure out what you're thinking in the process of having the conversation itself, rather than starting out with a set of views and then constructing a conversation to convey those thoughts?

Alison: Yes, though we had to begin with some relatively fixed ideas, none was guaranteed safe passage. I find that the process itself helps me to think more clearly and empathetically. Dialogue is a method, not merely a vehicle.

Reader: So those many seeming digressions, and the sometimes meandering quality of the text – they were intentional explorations?

Jules: You never find anything unexpected or new if you don't stray from the beaten track!

Russell: I've always been fond of tracks myself, rail and otherwise, but I will concede that the dialogical process has been eye-opening for me in a number of ways. I think Alison and Jules may be right that it facilitates encounters with ideas that essays can't so readily accomplish. And it may also be an archetype of effective teaching, so a dialogue on this particular subject self-reflexively compounds its effect.

Alternatives to Compulsory Schooling?

Reader: Perhaps so, if teaching itself is a kind of dialogue with students. But Russell, I have a question for you, or maybe more of a complaint. You several times rail against the ills of compulsory schooling, but you never even begin to explain what you would put in its place, or how a complex, modern society could function without supporting a fairly high level of universal education.

Russell: I plead guilty as charged. I suspect you have identified one of my weaknesses – an area in which I am almost as idealistic as my friend Jules here. I don't really think it would be healthy to abandon universal education wholesale, but I am certain it could and ought to take many creative forms beyond our rigid lockstep of K-12, or worse K-16.

Jules: That's music to my ears, Russell! If we were to rethink the structure of learning in our culture we'd be here a very long time, but I believe our conversation has identified some of the principles that should guide us. The goals of student dignity and autonomy, empathetic imagination, collaborative rather than competitive engagement, the importance of curiosity and other internal motivations, learning for life rather than just training for a job…

Alison: You'll have plenty to do designing educational experiences and institutions that honor these insights. We didn't want to hog all the fun!

Reader: Well, thanks. Very thoughtful of you.

Alison: Just doing our jobs.

How can we Become Ourselves?

Reader: Here's another question. The three of you speak a great deal in Chapter Six about character development, maturity, integrity, and so forth. The idea of growth or development of a self seems to rest, paradoxically, on the notion of a self that is already formed and persists through the changes. When I grow or change, it is *I* who grows and changes, after all.

Alison: Well, I'm glad at least that you're not confining yourself to *easy* questions!

Russell: This one's easy enough. The direct answer is no: none of our statements about character need presuppose a fixed or unchanging ontology of the self. Of course, as embodied minds, the physical structures that underlie reflective thought are sufficiently durable that when our personalities change they generally do so slowly.

Jules: Technicalities aside, I think Russell's basically right. As a matter of psychological observation, the main features of most people's personalities are fairly stable, though of course we can gradually grow and change over time. The conceit of teaching is the belief that sometimes others can direct that change in a way that *helps people evolve into themselves*.

Alison: What I suspect Jules means by that paradoxical phrase is that a person whose skills and character have developed to the point of enabling her to think and act autonomously is more integrated and empowered, hence a more complete and aware self.[85]

---

[85] For a detailed discussion of these issues see Robert Kegan, *The Evolving Self; Problem and Process in Human Development*.

Reader: I see. So since integrity comes in degrees, there's no absurdity in claiming both that everyone is already a developed self, and that the further integration of the self is an important aim.

Alison: Nicely put.

Isn't Philosophy Competitive?

Reader: Thank you. I have to say again that I have really enjoyed following your thoughtful conversations, and I find much wisdom in what you say, though of course I don't agree with all of it…

Russell: We would all be shocked and even a little disappointed if you did. We crave your comprehension of course, but we hope you'll agree with us only when we're right – and we don't even agree with each other much of the time! Sometimes the best we can manage is a small bridge connecting our views, rather than solid common ground.

Reader: Well, you seem to do pretty well in accommodating each others' perspectives. I was frankly a little surprised by this. I expected a philosophical conversation to be more fiercely competitive in defense of competing doctrines.

Alison: Jules, didn't we deal with that to some extent when we discussed the contrast between Socratic inquiry and sophistic dispute?

Jules: I think so, Alison. It also came up in relation to your highly competitive student. But throughout the conversation, I think you in particular, more than either Russell or I, have modeled a certain spirit of reconciliation that you perceive at the core of both teaching and philosophical inquiry.

Alison: I'm afraid I embody the spirit of reconciliation, as you put it, to the point of being positively annoying about it. It's been suggested I change my name to Pollyanna.

Russell: A rare intrusion of the passive voice there, Alison. Who would make that rude suggestion?

Alison: I'm just saying.

Jules: The point is that the popular image of intellectual combativeness is an unfortunate stereotype based on flawed characters and worldviews, rather than a feature of the best sort of inquiry. Even my spell-checking program seems to understand the ongoing struggle to outgrow our childish impulses – it recently suggested "flaw-sufferers" when I had typed "philosophers."

Russell: I like it. "We Who Suffer Flaws." Could I borrow that as the title of my next book?

Memorization *and* Creativity?

Reader: Now you guys are just being silly, so I'll ask my next question. You suggest at some point that memorizing things and practicing skills is compatible with and necessary for creativity, and that teaching is an improvisational art. I'm still a little puzzled about how these things fit together.

Alison: Creativity and improvisation are at the heart of teaching for me, and second only to music in the satisfaction I get from them.

Reader: Isn't that another way to undermine the view that teaching is merely a kind of paternalistic indoctrination? Since teachers are always learning, improvising, or developing creative strategies as they go, they stand to benefit *as thinkers* from teaching critical thinking.

Alison: That's an inference we were reaching for, I think, though none of us may have stated it so directly.

Jules: Makes perfectly good sense to me. I think even Russell could appreciate the movement between those flashes of insight he sometimes has while lecturing and later critical evaluations of them.

Russell: I admit I have sometimes thought better of ideas that I mistook for genius in the heat of discovery. You may also have experienced, Jules, the sudden shock of realizing that you have been presenting a concept for years without really understanding it. Thinking and learning are never perfect or complete, and teachers who think they're done with them have no business in the classroom.

Jules: I agree. At that point they are indoctrinators, not teachers, and the sworn enemies of student autonomy.

Reader: Yes, but I don't see how this answers my question.

Alison: We get a little carried away sometimes. I take your question to assume that studying and memorizing content are at odds with creativity and improvisation. Our discussion suggests the contrary: as in making music, training, practice, and memorization are the necessary *basis* of any fruitful creativity. You need good tools and lots of background to discover anything new or valuable.

Reader: If only schools made that connection! If there were more playfulness in learning content, hinting at the creative possibilities it will eventually open up for students, school wouldn't be such awful drudgery!

Alison: I doubt if you'll hear any quibbles with that suggestion from this crew.

Personal Strategies for Structural Problems?

Reader: For much of the conversation, you're trying to figure out how to foster autonomy by principled paternalistic means, because you can't envision another way to do it. But I wonder whether the problem only appears so difficult because you are seeking an individual solution to a systemic and pervasive problem of anti-intellectual, consumerist complacency.

Jules: I'm more than sympathetic to this sort of analysis, and I do think the structural ills in our culture seriously aggravate the tension. I am certain that in a healthy society, active curiosity would drive almost all learning, and the task of a teacher would be to supply tools, structure, the wisdom of experience when asked, and then get out of the way.

Alison: Jules's is a beautiful image, and between the best students and the best teachers there is already a synergy of this sort. I have to turn the question back to you, though, for other than looking for ways to inspire students to think well and critically for themselves, and find their own inner sources of curiosity, I don't have a clue how to go about healing the culture.

Russell: Right. And as I've always thought, *those who can, teach.*

Reader: That is a teacher's way of trying to change the world, I suppose, and I have to admit that I don't have any better ideas up my sleeve. But what you've just said anticipates my last question.

Alison: What's that?

To Teach or Not to Teach?

Reader: This may sound a little silly, but I have gotten to know enough about each of you that I'm now really curious about your decisions. Will you all go on teaching?

Russell: I can only speak for myself on that score, and in my case the answer is a good Aristotelian one: on the one hand yes, and on the other hand no.

Reader: Well, that's certainly satisfies my curiosity!

Russell: Glad to be of service. And thanks for the coffee.

Alison: Pay him no mind, he's a Trickster, or at least a joker. You were going to elaborate, weren't you, Russell?

Russell: If you insist. I've given the matter considerable thought, and our exploration of some of the key principles and difficulties of teaching has indeed focused my mind. On the one hand, I feel better prepared than ever to do battle with the dragons and demons of the classroom, without sacrificing all of my dignity. I feel it would be a shame to stop now.

Jules: And on the other hand? Now I'm as curious as our reader is!

Russell: Well I'm really not getting any younger, and I have things I want to accomplish, as I've mentioned, that are difficult to pursue on a full teaching schedule. So my plan is to approach my Dean about the possibility of a reduced teaching load, with a commensurate reduction in salary. I'm thinking maybe teaching a course or two each semester will keep me alive and honest, without running me ragged.

Conclusion

Jules: I hope that works out for you. I find that any teaching at all can expand to fill whatever time you have available.

Russell: I'm pretty sure I can manage. In any case, I want the engagement with students to stimulate and deepen my scholarly work – and my life.

Reader: That sounds like a compromise that might work, Russell. How about you, Jules?

Jules: I was afraid you'd ask me next. I wish I could tell you what I plan to do.

Reader: So you can't make up your mind?

Jules: I will always be a teacher of one sort or another, I have no doubt. It's just who I am. But of what sort, of what subject, in what institutional context – all this continues to bedevil me. Meanwhile I still have to earn my keep, so for the time being I will be returning to the trenches, armed with the thoughts and ideas we've shared, and less disheartened for having such good friends with whom to talk it through.

Reader: I have the impression from teachers I have known that collegial friendships, along with basic institutional support, make all the difference between sanity and its opposite.

Alison: I can heartily attest to that!

Reader: And what about you, Alison? Will you audition for the orchestra, and could you leave the classroom if they offer you a position?

Alison: If my brush with philosophy has taught me one thing, it's that the root of wisdom lies in acknowledging the limits of what I know. The answer to your question is one of the things I do not know.

Reader: I understand how much you love making music, Alison, but my impression is that you must be absolutely wonderful as a teacher – your thoughtfulness, patience, humor, and passion for literature and for learning are palpable. I just think it would be a huge loss for you to leave the profession!

Alison: I appreciate your vote of confidence, but as my mother liked to say, We'll See.

Reader: "We'll See?" I can't believe that's your answer.

Alison: Let me be clear that the opportunity to teach is among the greatest of privileges. The same features that make it frustrating also ensure that it's never boring, and the potential rewards – actually witnessing and participating in the joy of discovery, the realization of an ability newly acquired – are unlike nearly anything else in the world.

Reader: Yes, I understand this is how you view teaching, which is why I'm having trouble accepting your claim not to know what you'll do.

Alison: The unknown factor is basically a matter of faith.

Russell: Faith? You astonish me! I wasn't aware you were religious.

Alison: I didn't say that I was.

Jules: I'll bet I know what she means. The Greek term usually translated as 'faith' in the New Testament is *pistis*, and its root meaning is trust.[86] You're talking about being able to rely on your efforts being worthwhile in the face of limited evidence that you're making a difference, aren't you?

---

86 The Biblical use of *pistis* emphasizes this need for trust or confidence in the absence of concrete evidence, as in Thessalonians 3:2.

Alison: That is a teacher's faith. We relate to students at a certain stage in their lives, normally seeing very little of what it does for them, as if we were painting on barely visible canvases, each brushstroke nearly vanishing as we apply it. Once in a while we hear from a grateful student, but we never see the vast majority of what we accomplish, or know for sure that we accomplish much of anything.

Reader: So you're uncertain about continuing to teach because you may be losing your faith?

Alison: A musical performance is ephemeral, but at least in that moment I can hear what I'm doing, and whether I'm doing it well. Whatever an audience might think, I can experience directly even partial musical success, which is an end in itself.

Jules: But since teaching is essentially a relationship, you only succeed if your students do, which is very hard to discern, and may not even manifest until years later.

Russell: I don't see that it's a big problem. If they do reasonably well on the exams I give them, I can tell students are getting what I have to offer.

Jules: But Russell, I thought we agreed that objective content is only the raw material for learning as such, which involves creativity and transformation of the self. Our society tends to think about learning in that reductive way, but teachers know how much more there is to it.

Russell: Well, you know what they say about old dogs. It takes me awhile to change my habits of thought, and meantime I can tell myself I'm doing a good job without having to worry so much. Maybe my own faith is an ignorant, literalist one.

Alison: That's one comforting strategy, of course, though long term I doubt if it's very healthy.

Reader: Well I, for one, sincerely hope you are able to find and maintain your faith as a teacher, Alison.

Russell: I will second that with enthusiasm, and I trust Jules will do so as well.

Alison: I thank you all again for your confidence. And we'll see.

Epilogue

Alison, Russell, and Jules have evolved over the course of these conversations, now spanning two books, in ways we neither expected nor planned. Dialogue is good for us all, fictional persons included. In the process of outsourcing our thinking to this team of imaginary figures, our views on matters of knowledge and education have undergone similar transformations.

Therefore, it seems worth reminding readers that our present thoughts about teaching and learning are distinct from those of the characters. Alison's considered judgments most frequently resemble ours, but more generally our views emerge from the conversation as a whole.

There inevitably remain incomplete or erroneous moments of perceptivity, reasoning, and expression. Some of these belong to the characters by design, whereas some no doubt reflect the authors' present limitations.

One of the authors (Silliman) is indebted to Massachusetts College of liberal Arts for sabbatical leave during the 2010-11 academic year, and to St. Mary's College of Maryland for a visiting professorship. Thanks also to students participating in the authors' seminars on philosophy of education in the fall (St. Mary's) and spring (MCLA) of that year.

For graciously reading characters' parts at presentations of chapters in progress, our thanks to Sharon Wyrrick, Michael Taber, Nancy Snow, and James Boettcher.

Several friends and colleagues provided kind words of encouragement and offered to read early drafts. We wish to thank Gerol Petruzella, Jacob Wheeler, Susan Edgerton, Shelby Giaccarini, Nate Thorn, Bob Horn, Nicole Braden, Paul Nnodim, Bill Lawson, Chuck Stine, and Warren Blumenfeld.

And finally, we are especially grateful to Kathy Johnson, Sharon Wyrrick, and Keane Lundt for their perceptive, line-by-line editing. The book is much improved as a result of their efforts.

Bibliography

Aristophanes. *The Clouds*. William Arrowsmith, trans. Mentor, 1970. (Originally performed in 423 b.c.e.)

Aristotle, *Complete Works*. Princeton University Press, 1984.

Bateson, Mary Catherine. *Peripheral Visions: Learning Along the Way*. Harper Collins, 1994.

Bell, Clive. "Art as Significant Form." In: *The Nature of Art*, Tom Wartenburg, Ed. Harcourt College Publishers, 2002.

Burbules, Nicholas C., and Rupert Berk. "Critical Thinking and Critical Pedagogy: Relations, Differences, and Limits." In *Critical Theories in Education*, Thomas S. Popkewitz and Lynn Fendler, eds., Routledge, 1999. (Available online.)

Carroll, Lewis (Dodson, Charles L.). *The Works of Lewis Carroll*. Paul Hamlyn, 1965.

Dickens, Charles. *Hard Times*. Simon & Schuster, 2007. (Originally published in 1854.)

Dutton, Denis. *The Art Instinct*. Bloomsbury Press, 2010.

Freire, Paulo. *Pedagogy of the Oppressed*. Continuum, 2000 (Originally published in 1970.)

Gardner, Howard. *Multiple Intelligences*. Basic Books, 2006.
Glasersfeld, Ernst von. "An Introduction to Radical

Constructivism." In *The Invented Reality*, P. Watzlawick, ed. Norton, 1984. (Available online.)

Gopnik, Alison. *The Philosophical Baby*. Picador, 2010.

Griswold, Charles. *Platonic Writings, Platonic Readings*. Pennsylvania State University Press, 2001.

Havelock, Eric. *Preface to Plato*. Belknap Press, 1982.

Heath, Chip, and Dan Heath. *Made to Stick; Why Some Ideas Die and Others Survive*. Random House, 2007.

Hume, David. *An Enquiry Concerning Human Understanding*. Oxford University Press, 1975. (Originally published in 1787.)

Hyde, Lewis. *Trickster Makes This World; Mischief, Myth, and Art*. Farrar, Strauss & Giroux, 2010.

James, William. *Principles of Psychology*. Cosimo Classics, 2007.

Johnson, David Kenneth, and Matthew R. Silliman. *Bridges to the World; A Dialogue on the Construction of Knowledge, Education, and Truth*. Sense Publishers, 2009.

Kant, Immanuel. *Critique of Pure Reason*. Norman Kemp Smith, Trans., St. Martin's Press, 1965. (originally published in 1787.)

Kant, Immanuel. *Foundations of the Metaphysics of Morals*. Lewis White Beck, Trans., Library of Liberal Arts, 1976. (Originally published in 1785.)

Kalkavage, Peter. "The Neglected Muse: Why Music is an Essential Liberal Art." *American Educator*, Fall 2006. (Available online.)

Kegan, Robert. *The Evolving Self; Problem and Process in Human Development*. Harvard University Press, 1982.

Keller, Evelyn Fox. *A Feeling for the Organism The Life and Work of Barbara McClintock*. W.H. Freeman, 1984.

Kolb, D.A. *Experiential Learning: Experience as the Source of Learning and Development*. Prentice-Hall, 1984.

Levitin, Daniel J. *This is Your Brain on Music*. Plume/Penguin, 2007.

Locke, John. *Two Treatises of Government*. Cambridge University Press, 1960. (Originally published 1790.)

Maturana, Umberto. "Reality: The Search for Objectivity or the Quest for a Compelling Argument." *Irish Journal of Psychology*, Vol. 9 No. 1, 1998, pp. 25-82.

Montuori, Alfonso. "The Complexity of Improvisation and the Improvisation of Complexity: Social Science, Art, and Complexity." *Human Relations*, 2003. (Available online.)

Nagel, Thomas. *The View From Nowhere*. Oxford University Press, 1989.

Nussbaum, Martha. *For Profit; Why Democracy Needs the Humanities*. Princeton University Press, 2010.

Plato. *Complete Works*. Hackett, 1997.
Postman, Neil. *The End of Education*. Vintage, 1996.

Rifkin, Jeremy. *The Empathic Civilization*. Jeremy P. Tarcher / Penguin, 2009.

Sayre, Kenneth. *Plato's Literary Garden*. University of Notre Dame Press, 2002.

Scheffler, Israel. *The Language of Education*. Charles C. Thomas, 1960.

Siegel, Harvey. *Educating Reason*. Routledge, 1988.

Siegel, Harvey. "Gimme That Old-Time Enlightenment Meta-Narrative: Radical Pedagogies (And Politics) Require Old-Fashioned Epistemology (And Moral Theory)." *Inquiry: Critical Thinking Across the Disciplines*, 11, 4, 1993. (reprinted in *Rationality Redeemed?*)

Siegel, Harvey. *Rationality Redeemed?* Routledge, 1996.

Silliman, Matthew R. *Sentience and Sensibility; a conversation about moral philosophy*. Parmenides Publishing, 2006.

Stove, David. *The Plato Cult*. Wiley-Blackwell, 1991.

Suber, Peter. "Paternalism," in Christopher B. Gray ed., *Philosophy of Law: An Encyclopedia*. Garland Publishing Co, 1999, II, pp. 632-635.

Thaler, Richard H., and Cass R. Sunstein. *Nudge*. Penguin Books, 2008.

Walder, Andrew G. *Fractured Rebellion: The Beijing Red Guard Movement*. Harvard University Press, 2010.

Whitehead, Alfred North. *The Aims of Education*. Free Press, 1967. (Originally published in 1929.)

Wolff, Tobias. *Old School*. Vintage Books, 2003.

Wyman, Max. *The Defiant Imagination: Why Culture Matters*. Douglas and McIntyre, 2004.

Xenophon. *The Memorable Thoughts of Socrates*. Grizzell, 2010.

Zull, James. *The Art of Changing the Brain*. Stylus Publishing, 2002.

Index

active learning, 3, 4, 12, 33, 34, 36, 38, 40, 148
aporia, 94, 94n, 95, 105-6, 114
Aristotle, 102, 102n, 103n
authority, ix, 1-21, 43, 49-51, 55, 64, 113-5, 131
autonomy, viii, 1, 1n, 12-17, 19-20, 35, 47-8, 55, 55-7, 64, 72, 77, 80-1, 91, 125-6, 129, 140, 143, 147-8

Bateson, Mary Catherine, 85, 85n
Bell, Clive, 74, 74n
Bennett, William, 127n
Burbules, Nicholas C., 52n

Carroll, Lewis, 100n
character
    literary, 91-6, 104, 107n, 110, 120, 128, 155
    moral, ix, 23, 28, 96, 105, 119-36, 144, 146
Chopin, 137
competition, 134-6
compulsory schooling, 2, 4, 26, 35, 143
constructivism:
    radical, 3, 41-2, 44, 53, 53n
content
    artistic, 72, 74-5, 80
    pedagogical, viii, 5, 28n, 49, 52, 63-4, 66, 87, 90, 96, 119, 121-2, 124, 147, 152
creativity, x, 18, 33, 39, 69-87, 103, 111-2, 134, 143, 146-7, 152
critical thinking, viii, 47-66, 73-85, 91-2, 95, 109, 111, 116, 120, 123, 126, 128-9, 146, 148
curiosity, 27, 31, 95, 101n, 115, 132, 136, 141, 143, 148-9

Dewey, John, 30
dialogue, vii, x, 20, 47n, 80, 89, 92-3, 93n, 94n, 98, 100n, 105, 105n, 112-4, 120, 120n, 132, 134, 140n, 141-3, 155
Dickens, Charles, 14n, 21
Dutton, Denis, 70, 70n, 77
deception, 91, 104-5, 107, 112

emotion, 13-4, 36, 38, 63-4, 81, 100-1, 103, 121, 128
empathy, ix, 23, 43, 57n, 62, 86, 102, 120, 128, 142, 143
ethics, 47, 79, 98, 102n
etymology, 19, 31, 123

faith, 69, 151-2
fallibility, 41-4, 54. 120-1
feelings, 28, 34n, 43, 44n, 97n, 101-2, 128-9, 135
Freire, Paulo, 47-8, 50-2, 55-66, 109, 111, 125

Gardner, Howard, 43, 43n
Glasersfeld, Ernst von, 42n
Gopnik, Alison, 37n, 107n
Griswold, Charles, 105n

Havelock, Eric, 98n
Heath, Chip, and Dan Heath, 62n
Hume, David, 54
Hyde, Lewis, 111n

imagination, ix, xi, 4, 15, 23, 62, 66, 69-72, 80-5, 89, 93, 94, 102-3, 107n, 107-8, 114n, 128, 129-30, 143, 155

indoctrination, 64, 111, 124, 125-6, 146-7
improvisation, ix, 19, 23, 27, 39, 67-8, 69, 80-7, 132, 141, 146-7
integrity, 123, 144
intellectual virtues, 119, 121, 123-4, 130
interpretive charity, 99, 99n, 123-4

James, William, 44n
jazz, 39, 75, 80-2, 86, 137
Johnson, David Kenneth, 3n, 40n, 53n
justice, 47-66, 78, 96-7, 101-2

Kant, Immanuel, 19, 19n, 28, 28n, 65, 65n
Kalkavage, Peter, 77n
Kegan, Robert, 144n
Keller, Evelyn Fox, 34n
knowledge, vii, 3, 3n, 25-8, 31, 33, 35, 40-4, 50, 53n, 54, 62, 65, 72, 94-5, 98-104, 109, 120, 126, 155
Kolb, D.A., 37n

learning
    as knowing that/ knowing how, 26-8, 103
    as consuming, 35-6
    as play, 70-1, 107, 115, 122, 129, 147

lecture, 20-1, 30-4, 41, 92, 96-7, 100, 104, 130
Levitin, Daniel J., 124n
liberation, 47, 50-2, 55-8, 61, 64, 77
Locke, John, 7, 7n, 35-6, 54

manipulation (see trickstser)
Maturana, Umberto, 35n
maturity, 1, 8, 13-5, 17, 20, 64, 81, 98, 100-2, 119, 131, 144
McClintock, Barbara, 34n, 109
memorization, 42, 69, 124, 129-30, 146, 147
meta-narrative, 34-5, 54n, 59, 59n
Montuori, Alfonso, 81n
Mozart, 38, 78-9
motivation, 2, 4, 6, 27, 33, 64, 67, 107, 133-6, 143

Nagel, Thomas, 52n
narrative/story, 23, 31, 62, 100, 108-9, 114, 128, 130-4
Nussbaum, Martha, 57n

objectivity, 5, 39, 49, 49n, 56, 59, 60n, 66, 119, 152

paradox, viii, 13, 18-9, 69, 81, 140n, 140-4
paternalism, 1-21, 50, 61, 105-7, 114, 127, 140, 146, 148
pedagogy, x, 11, 25, 30, 34, 36, 44, 47, 47n, 50-1, 52n, 54n, 55, 60-1, 64-5, 72, 76, 80, 89, 91, 93n, 94-9, 104, 109, 117, 125, 134-5, 140
Petrucciani, Michel, 86
Piaget, Jean, 36, 37n
Plato, 30, 53n, 89, 91-105, 108n, 110-3, 115, 119-21, 135
poiesia, 103
politics of education, 18, 48, 54-55, 111
Postman, Neil, 109n

realism, 40-1, 43, 44
reason, x, 11, 31, 37n, 47, 49-51, 56, 58-63, 80, 96-101, 104, 119, 124, 128-30
relativism, 42, 53-5
Rifkin, Jeremy, 57n
Rumsfeld, Donald, 13, 13n

Sayre, Kenneth, 115n
Scheffler, Israel, 104n
Siegel, Harvey, 54n, 59n, 82n, 128-9

Silliman, Matthew R., 3n, 40n, 53n,
  79n
Socrates, 91-116, 120-1, 132, 135, 142,
  145
Stove, David, 53n
Suber, Peter, 8n
sunousia, 96-7, 96n, 97n
Sunstein, Cass R., 19n

taste, 49n, 70-1, 74, 76-80
teacher-student relationship, 1n, 14,
  50-1, 54, 86, 89, 96, 125, 134, 152
Thaler, Richard H., 19n
trickster, ix, 109-12, 113n, 114n, 115,
  131, 136, 149
trust, 104, 106-7, 151, 151n, 153

understanding, viii, 5, 13, 16-8, 23,
  25, 33, 37, 40-1, 44, 50, 53-5, 58n,
  61-2, 77, 78, 84, 94, 94n, 100-3, 106,
  107n, 1008, 110, 124, 134-6, 139
    as realization, 102-3, 121, 151

Walder, Andrew G., 125n
Whitehead, Alfred North, 36n, 58,
  58n, 87, 87n, 129, 130n
Wolff, Tobias, 129n
Wyman, Max, 71-2, 72n, 82

Xenophon, 93n

Zull, James, 37n

www.ingramcontent.com/pod-product-compliance
Lightning Source LLC
LaVergne TN
LVHW020930090426
835512LV00020B/3292